Why Eve Doesn't Have an Adam's Apple
A Dictionary of Sex Differences

Why Eve Doesn't Have an Adam's Apple
A Dictionary of Sex Differences

Carol Ann Rinzler

☑® Facts On File, Inc.

AN INFOBASE HOLDINGS COMPANY

What are little boys made of?
Snips and snails, and puppy dogs' tails;
That's what little boys are made of.

What are little girls made of?
Sugar and spice, and everything nice;
That's what little girls are made of.
                                    —Traditional nursery rhyme

The material in this book, which was current at the time the book was written, is intended for your information only. It is not meant to be a substitute for consulting with your own physician. All matters regarding your health require medical supervision.

Why Eve Doesn't Have an Adam's Apple: A Dictionary of Sex Differences

Copyright © 1996 by Carol Ann Rinzler

Facts On File, Inc.
11 Penn Plaza
New York, NY 10001

Library of Congress Cataloging-in-Publication Data
Rinzler, Carol Ann.
    Why Eve doesn't have an Adam's apple : a dictionary of sex
differences / Carol Ann Rinzler
        p. cm.
    Includes bibliographical references and index.
    ISBN 0-8160-3356-0 (pbk)
    ISBN 0-8160-3352-8 (hc)
    1. Sex differences—Dictionaries.   I. Title.
QP81.5.R56   1996
612.6—dc20   95-43133

Facts On File books are available at special discounts when purchased in bulk quantities for businesses, associations, institutions or sales promotions. Please call our Special Sales Department in New York at 212/967-8800 or 800/322-8755.

Layout by Robert Yaffe
Cover design by Leah Lococo

This book is printed on acid-free paper.
Printed in the United States of America

MP 10 9 8 7 6 5 4 3 2 1

CONTENTS

A NOTE TO THE READER

Throughout this book, there are numerous references to "men," "women," "a man," "a woman," "male," and "female." In each case, the term refers to an average man or woman. Clearly, individuals can (and do) vary from this theoretical norm.

Under several entries for major diseases and causes of death, you may find two charts, the first showing reported deaths or cases in 1991, the second the number of deaths or cases estimated to occur in 1992. These figures represent the latest information available at the time this book was written. The first is a known quantity, the second a projection. Both are included to show trend lines.

In many entries, there are words set in small capitals: for example, SEBA-CEOUS GLANDS. This is a cross-reference to an entry with this heading.

INTRODUCTION

Somebody sneezed in a dusty house. Was it more likely to be a man or a woman?

If you said "a man," you're right. According to the National Center for Health Statistics, men are about 20 percent more likely than women to be sensitive to house dust.

Another way to tell men and women apart is to listen to their hearts. On average, *hers* beats slightly faster than *his*, even before birth. You might also check out who's sleeping in this morning: the National Bureau of Economic Research says that women sleep slightly longer than men. Women also live longer, and when seriously ill, seem able to postpone dying long enough to celebrate a meaningful anniversary. Men are more likely to expire right before a birthday.

Men and women, though equal, are clearly not the same. Their bodies and their minds diverge, and not simply in the obvious physical aspects such as breasts and penis.

Blame the differences on testis determining factor (TDF), a gene or group of genes on the Y chromosome.

In describing how computers work, hackers sometimes talk about the "default mode"—the way things go if nobody tinkers with the basic program.

That's pretty much how human beings become either male or female.

As a general rule, each of us has 48 chromosomes. Forty-six of them—the *autosomes*—determine characteristics other than gender. The other two chromosomes, the X chromosome and the Y chromosome, decide whether we are male or female.

Everyone has one X chromosome, the default mode. Females have a second X chromosome; no disruption there. But males have one X chromosome and one Y chromosome. The Y chromosome changes the program.

For the first few weeks of pregnancy, XX embryos and XY embryos develop in precisely the same way, with identical rudimentary structures that will eventually differentiate into organs and tissues. Minus the Y chromosome, every embryo's sex organs would be female, but sometime in the seventh week—some say precisely on the 40th day after conception—TDF kicks in. After that, nothing is the same.

Now the XY fetal tissues are bathed in testosterone, not estrogen, and visible differences emerge—external rather than internal sex organs; longer, heavier male bones versus the broader, shallower female pelvis. In the brain, subtler differences arise as neurons create linkages that will encourage different ways of thinking, perhaps a male facility with numbers versus a female affinity for language and speech.

By the time the child emerges from the womb, TDF has done its work. There is no escaping the very real differences between the sexes.

Identifying and explaining gender differences is more than a parlor game.

It is the key to vital medical secrets, explaining, among other things, why women are less likely to suffer from heart disease and cancer, and why men accept organ transplants more readily.

In a consumer society, our differences also have economic implications. It's no accident that there are "dress shields" for women but no "shirt shields" for men, or that women's winter gloves are more likely to be lined with wool or fur. Both men and women perspire, but in different amounts at different places on the body. Both men and women experience the extremes of temperature, but what one perceives as too hot or too cold, the other may quite naturally find comfortably warm or cool.

For a long time, it has been possible to measure bones and muscle and to use this information to compensate for the different physical abilities of men and women in similar kinds of work. Now, advanced technologies give us extraordinary imaging techniques that let us watch the living brain at work, to see with our own eyes, or visualize from the words and pictures of medical researchers, the different ways in which men and women think and reason.

In themselves, our differences are neither good nor bad.

It is what we make of them—how we use our gifts—that counts.

A

accidents   Accidents are unplanned, unexpected, unpleasant, and (no surprise here) much more common among males in all age groups except the very old.

Tempting as it may be to blame this on an inherent male awkwardness, the fact is that our society encourages risky behavior in males that it discourages in females, and this risky behavior often leads to accidental injury and death. As medical care and sanitary practices have improved, deaths from infection have declined. Perhaps as a result, accidents are now the leading cause of death among people younger than 15, killing more children than cancer, birth defects, respiratory infections, and heart disease combined. For every fatal injury, another 1,000 children are seriously hurt.

The most common accidental injury among children is a fall in the home, including a fall from an open window. A recent law requiring gates on all apartment windows in New York City reduced deaths from window falls by more than 90 percent in one year.

REPORTED DEATHS FROM ACCIDENTS, 1991		
Age	Male	Female
All ages (yrs.)	59,730	29,617
1–14	4,059	2,266
15–34	23,100	6,944
35–54	14,194	4,695
55–74	9,472	5,221
75+	8,234	10,073

Source: National Center for Health Statistics, *Vital Statistics of the United States, 1991* (Washington, D.C.: Public Health Service, 1994).

ESTIMATED DEATHS FROM ACCIDENTAL INJURY, 1992		
Age	**Male**	**Female**
Less than 1 yr.	420	430
1–14	3,960	1,900
15–24	10,530	3,390
25–34	10,380	3,140
35–44	8,550	2,620
45–54	5,120	2,040
55–64	4,350	2,280
65–74	4,940	3,300
75–84	5,230	4,680
85+	3,480	5,240

Source: U.S. Centers for Disease Control, "Provisional numbers of deaths for the 10 leading causes of death by age, race and sex, United States, 1992," *Monthly Vital Statistics*, September 28, 1993.

Car accidents are a second important cause of accidental death among the young, accounting for 40 deaths every year for every 100,000 Americans age 15 to 24. Accidents were also the leading cause of death among young adults, age 25 to 44, until 1992 when AIDS moved into first place.

achondroplasia   An inherited form of dwarfism caused by a failure of cartilage to convert to bone. Achondroplasic dwarfs have a normal-size trunk, but their arms and legs are shorter than normal. Achondroplasia is an example of a BIRTH DEFECT caused by a single gene; it is more common among children born to older fathers.

acne   Neither sex escapes the spots of adolescence, but boys are more likely than girls to suffer from severe widespread acne.

In both boys and girls, acne is a response to rising levels of androgens (male hormones), specifically testosterone, at puberty. Androgens stimulate the SEBACEOUS GLANDS to produce sebum, an oily, waxy material that prevents the evaporation of water from the surface of the skin, thus keeping the skin soft and supple. But sebum also blocks pores, creating an environment in which the bacteria that cause acne infections can flourish. Acne is worse among adolescent boys because of their naturally higher testosterone levels, but acne scars—the residue of old lesions—seem to be equally common among adult men and women.

Exposure to sunlight may also trigger acne. So may certain cosmetic ingredients that clog the pores. To avoid this, it makes sense to choose cosmetic

---

COSMETIC INGREDIENTS THAT MAY CAUSE BLACKHEADS AND WHITEHEADS

butyl stearate	myristal lactate
cocoa butter	myristyl myristate
decyl oleate	octyl palmitate
grape seed oil	octyl stearate and derivatives
isocetyl stearate	oleic acid
isopropyl myristate	oleyl alcohol
isopropyl palmitate	olive oil
isostearyl neopentanoate	peanut oil
lanolin	petrolatum
laureth-4	propylene glycol
linseed oil	stearate
mineral oil	sesame oil
myristal ether propionate	sodium lauryl sulfate

Source: Andrew Scheman and David Severson, *Cosmetics Buying Guide*, (Consumer Reports Books, 1994).

---

products whose ingredients are described on the label as "noncomedogenic." These are unlikely to block the pores and create comedones (blackheads and whiteheads) that can turn into acne lesions.

aging   As they age, both men and women experience a variety of changes in body and mind, but they do not necessarily experience them at the same time or to the same extent. Women, for example, lose more bone density faster and are therefore at greater risk of OSTEOPOROSIS, while men lose more BRAIN CELLS and may experience a greater diminution of their LANGUAGE AND SPEECH skills. Which changes affect whom and how fast they occur is generally (but not always) determined by the SEX HORMONES, testosterone and estrogen.

AIDS (acquired immune deficiency syndrome)   AIDS is a secondary immune deficiency syndrome, one of the consequences of an HIV INFECTION. In the early years of the epidemic, AIDS was spread primarily through male homosexual contact.

In 1992, AIDS became the leading killer of American men age 25 to 44. Today, however, heterosexual infection and infection via sharing of needles has made AIDS the fourth leading cause of death among women in this age group, behind cancer, accidents, and heart disease. Nationwide the incidence of new

---

AGE-RELATED CHANGES IN THE BODY: MEN VERSUS WOMEN

Change	Who Is More Severely Affected
Loss of brain cells	Men
Dimming vision	Women
Gray hair	Both
Excess growth of eyelashes and eyebrows	Both
Loss of facial hair	Men
Growth of facial hair	Women
Loss of body hair	Both
Thinning skin	Women
Dry skin	Women
Decrease in perspiration	Both
Decline in secretion of sex hormones	Women
Degeneration of germ cells	Both
Loss of bone density	Women
Loss of height	Both
Spreading feet	Both

See entries on beard; body odor; cataract; eyebrows and eyelashes; feet; fertility; germ cells; hair; hair, graying; height; high blood pressure; hip; infertility; language and speech; macular degeneration; osteoporosis; perspiration; sebaceous glands; sex hormones; wrinkles.

---

cases of AIDS among women is rising at the rate of roughly 17 percent a year. In 1995, the Centers for Disease Control in Atlanta predicted that within three years, AIDS would be the second leading cause of death among young adult women.

Once diagnosed with AIDS, women appear to die twice as quickly as men, perhaps because they are likely to be diagnosed later in the course of the disease. A woman's symptoms—recurrent vaginal infections, chronic pelvic inflammatory disease, severe genital herpes—may not fit the classic AIDS picture based on the early, almost exclusively male experience with the disease. In addition, when women suffer symptoms such as weight loss, HEADACHE, and fatigue, doctors may improperly diagnose the symptoms as psychological problems, and miss the infectious disease.

alcohol, effects on reproduction   Alcohol abuse affects both male and female reproductive function. The most obvious effect of alcohol on men is the inability to attain or sustain an erection, a situation once known as "brewer's droop," presumably in honor of those for whom it was an occupational hazard. Men who abuse alcohol may have lower testosterone levels; some laboratory studies show that animals who are given large amounts of alcohol are infertile or sire offspring with developmental problems.

In one 12-year series of such experiments by Robert A. Anderson Jr., associate professor of obstetrics and gynecology research at Rush Presbyterian St. Luke's Medical Center in Chicago, the male mice were able to impregnate the females, but litters were smaller than expected and up to 80 percent of the pups died within a month of weaning. A 1986 University of Washington survey of 377 Seattle infants suggested that babies born to men who were "regular drinkers" (two glasses of table wine or one bottle of beer or one ounce of 100-proof whiskey on any one occasion, once a month) might weigh an average 6.5 ounces less than babies whose fathers consumed less alcohol. But these results, the first to link low BIRTH WEIGHT to a father's drinking, have never been replicated.

In 1994, Ricardo A. Yazigi of Temple University School of Medicine proposed a mechanism by which a man's use of drugs and alcohol may affect his offspring. Using sperm from human donors, Yazigi has shown that tiny specks of drugs such as cocaine attach themselves to specific sites on the sperm. The sperm then carry the drug—and any genetic damage—into an embryo. "It is probably wise for men to avoid cocaine and other drugs for some time around the period of conception," Yazigi says. "We have not established a time limit, so the longer the better."

Alcohol abuse does not make a woman infertile, but it may interfere with her ability to experience ORGASM. Alcohol abuse during PREGNANCY may cause fetal alcohol syndrome (FAS). This is a specific pattern of birth defects—low birth weight, heart defects, facial malformation, learning disabilities, and mental retardation—that sometimes occurs in infants born to alcoholic women who consume more than six drinks a day while pregnant. (One drink = 12 ounces of beer, 5 ounces of wine, or 1.25 ounces of distilled spirits.) Although many women may prefer to abstain completely while pregnant, there is no consistent data linking BIRTH DEFECTS to moderate consumption by women who do not abuse alcohol either before or during pregnancy.

alcohol, tolerance for   Some men and women are more sensitive than others to the effects of alcohol, but in general, men can drink more than women without showing ill effects.

This is due partly to differences in BODY COMPOSITION. There is more fluid in "active" tissue (muscle) than in "supporting tissue" (fat and bone). Because women have more FAT and less MUSCLE, they also have proportionately less water. This difference in the ratio of fat to muscle means that women do not dilute alcohol as efficiently as men.

In 1994, the National Institute on Alcohol Abuse and Alcoholism (NIAAA) funded a study at the Research Institute of Addictions in Buffalo, New York that showed that even when they take fewer drinks, women have more alcohol in their bodies. In interviews with 273 alcoholics who had stopped drinking and a control group of 133 moderate "social" drinkers, the researchers found that when they drank, the men and women in the control group reported consuming an average 3.8 and 2.4 drinks, respectively. But taking the differences in body fluid content into account, the amount of alcohol in the body was just about equal: an average 1.05 grams of alcohol per kilogram of body fluid for women versus 1.16 g/kg for the men. Among alcoholics, the ratio was even closer: 7.83 grams of alcohol per kilogram of body fluid for women; 7.65 g/kg for men.

Because the female body has less blood and other fluids to dissolve the alcohol, the women's reactions were more pronounced. "The brain doesn't count the number of drinks; it counts the number of alcohol molecules that reach it," pharmacologist and study leader James L. York told the *New York Times*.

A second reason why women react more strongly to alcohol is that they secrete smaller amounts of the enzymes needed to metabolize it. The stomach lining is dotted with small pits that lead to gastric glands that secrete enzymes, hydrochloric acid, mucus to protect the instestinal wall from the acid, and chemicals that trigger the release of digestive enzymes from the pancreas and gallbladder. Among the enzymes secreted by the gastric glands is alcohol dehydrogenase (ADH). The ADH secreted in the stomach metabolizes some of the alcohol a person consumes; the rest flows on to the liver, which produces its own form of ADH. Regardless of gender, the human body produces a limited amount of ADH in both the stomach and the liver. At any one time, there is less than the body needs to process all the alcohol in a single drink.

However in 1990, a team of researchers led by Dr. Charles S. Lieber of the Mount Sinai Medical (New York) Center and the Bronx Veterans Affairs Medical Center reported that women produce much less ADH, pound for pound, than men do. Generally, a man produces enough ADH to metabolize about 0.1 gram of pure alcohol for each 2.2 pounds (1 kilogram) of body weight an hour—about ¼ ounce (6.8 gm) for a 150-pound (68 kg) man. Women produce less ADH and metabolize less alcohol in any given time period. Any alcohol not metabolized either in the stomach or the liver flows out into the bloodstream, then circles back to the liver. This cycle is repeated as many times as required to metabolize all the alcohol a person has consumed. Because a woman metabolizes so little alcohol in her stomach, more pure alcohol goes to her liver and then out into her bloodstream. If a man and a woman each take one drink, there will be more pure alcohol circulating in the woman's body than in the man's.

Not only do men and women secrete different amounts of ADH, but they also secrete it on different time schedules. According to Kenneth Jon Rose, author of *The Body In Time*, the male liver secretes alcohol dehydrogenase most quickly and most copiously early in the morning, around 8 A.M. The female liver, on the other hand, churns out ADH fastest about five hours earlier, around 3 A.M.

altitude   Although human beings have been colonizing at high altitudes for centuries—Machu Picchu, Katmandu, and Winter Park, Colorado spring quickly to mind—their bodies live most comfortably at sea level. As the altitude increases, the amount of oxygen in the atmosphere decreases, and eventually the body revolts. At 6,500 feet above sea level, just about the altitude of Gallup, New Mexico, one may experience headache, a jumpy stomach, ringing ears, and an inability to catch one's breath. About 20 percent of those who climb to 9,000 feet will find their hearts beating irregularly and their limbs turning leaden. Their lungs may begin to swell and to leak bloody sputum, and their concentration will be disrupted by swelling in the brain. If they climb higher still, all these symptoms will get worse. Without prompt medical care, they may die.

Who is most at risk? The climber of either sex who ascends too rapidly, without stopping at each level to allow the body to acclimate itself to the reduced supply of oxygen. Premenstrual women may have special difficulty adjusting to high altitudes, perhaps because the progesterone-flooded body accumulates extra fluid in the last few days of the cycle.

The most interesting gender-related effect of high altitude may be its impact on the male reproductive system. Sperm production is a continuous and delicate process, sensitive to environmental influences such as changes in the amount of oxygen in the air. Studies show that as soon as three days after a man arrives at an elevation of 12,000 feet or higher, his testicles are producing testosterone at only half their normal rate. If he stays at that altitude for a week, his sperm count takes a nosedive to less than 50 percent of what he had at sea level; at two weeks, it is down to 30 percent. At the same time, there is an increase in the number of abnormally shaped sperm—sperm with two heads, two tails, no tail at all. By the end of a month, the ratio of normal to abnormal sperm is 50:50. Some experts calculate that men who have more than 30 percent to 40 percent abnormal sperm will be infertile. The situation is not irreversible though. It takes about two months to produce a mature sperm, so when climbers return to sea level their sperm counts (and morphology) gradually return to normal as the body continues to produce new sperm.

This may be one reason why the Spanish conquistadors, who marched through the Central and South American lowlands like a phalanx of General Shermans striding through Georgia, never actually conquered the mountain peoples of the South American Andes. Even after their bodies adjusted to the altitude, the would-be conquerors were less successful than the natives at reproduction, almost certainly because their ascent to the Andean heights reduced their supply of viable sperm. Unlike most conquering armies, therefore, they could not establish a continuing base of loyal families, and their control over the mountain territories ended as soon as they left.

Alzheimer's disease   A 1987 survey of Alzheimer's patients conducted at six diagnostic and treatment centers by University of Southern California scientists suggests that more than two-thirds of all Alzheimer's victims are women.

Is this because of a greater genetic predisposition to Alzheimer's in women or simply because they are more likely to live to the ripe old ages that make them candidates for this disabling disorder (see LIFE EXPECTANCY)?

The jury is still out on that one, but there is already evidence that female sex hormones may have a role to play in facilitating the production of critical enzymes in brain cells and maintaining the network of fibers that transmit neurological impulses from one nerve cell to the next. If this is true, then the decline in estrogen secretion at menopause might logically be thought to accelerate the kind of neuron and brain cell loss that characterizes Alzheimer's disease, eventually affecting cognition and memory.

One study of more than 2,000 California women has suggested that taking hormones at menopause might reduce a woman's risk of Alzheimer's by as much as 40 percent, and some researchers believe that taking estrogen may also improve memory function for women who have had their ovaries surgically removed. Barbara B. Sherwin, professor of psychology at McGill University in Montreal, has compared ten years' worth of data from two groups of such women, the first taking estrogen, the second a placebo. Based on the results of neurological tests, Sherwin concluded that women taking estrogen do better on tests of verbal memory. For example, their recall of whole paragraphs they had read was superior to that of women who did not use hormones. However, several later studies have failed to replicate Sherwin's results, showing no difference in memory function.

amyotropic lateral sclerosis (ALS)   ALS, the disease that killed New York Yankees first baseman Lou Gehrig in 1941, causes a progressive degeneration of nerve cells, leading to muscular weakness and atrophy that eventually leads to paralysis and death. There is as yet no scientific explanation for the often observed fact that men are more likely than women to be affected.

ankylosing spondylitis   Ankylosing spondylitis, also known as Strumpell-Marie disease for German physician Ernst Adolf von Strumpell and French neurologist Pierre Marie, who first identified it, is a form of arthritis that often runs in families, is more common among men, and may be transmitted by a dominant gene.

The symptoms are a stiffening (ankylosis) of a joint caused by a melding together (spondylitis) of fibers and bone.

anorexia nervosa   Anorexia nervosa is an EATING DISORDER characterized by the refusal to eat. People with anorexia nervosa hold a distorted view of their own bodies and have an overwhelming fear of obesity. They think of themselves as fat even when the scale registers "thin."

Most people with anorexia nervosa are women. In one recent study in Rochester, Minnesota, the incidence of anorexia nervosa per 100,000 people was estimated at about 270 females and 22 males. Overall, the incidence of anorexia among American women may run from one in every 100 to one in every 250. In the mid-1970s, a study among the privileged young women students in British private high schools produced similar results: approximately one of every 100 girls over the age of 16 was suffering from anorexia nervosa. (In British private and public schools combined, the number was one of every 250 girls.)

Anorexia is rare in places where food is scarce or in times of famine, but it is not a new disease. Anorexia nervosa in the form of uncontrolled fasting was first identified by physicians in England and France in the 1870s. It became faddishly popular in the years after World War II, when, as *New York Times* health columnist Jane E. Brody notes, there was a sudden, dramatic increase in the number of girls who learned about anorexia and 'choose' it to express their emotional and social turmoil."

There is no doubt that social and psychological factors can trigger anorexia—particularly the emphasis on the attractiveness of a thin, boyish body shape and the cultural disdain for fat bodies, which are associated with unpleasant and undesirable social, physical, and psychological characteristics. These attitudes are so deeply ingrained in the American social character that as many as 90 percent of all prepubertal children in the United States may already know that fat is regarded as unfavorable. More than 50 percent of young girls attempt to diet or otherwise control their weight. However, only a small percentage of them will go on to develop anorexia nervosa, so it is clear that other factors are at work.

For nearly 20 years it has been obvious that many anorectics share defects not only in appetite but in the ability to regulate body temperature, water balance, and hormone secretion, and that these problems last even after the anorexia has abated. Women with anorexia often fail to menstruate because their weight has fallen below that needed to maintain ovulation. But as psychologist Alexandra W. Logue of the State University of New York at Stony Brook has written, many female anorectics cease menstruating *before* they experience serious weight loss. This suggests a physical reason for both the anorexia and the failure to menstruate. The likeliest candidate is a dysfunctional hypothalamus—the gland that plays an important role both in eating behavior and in secretion of the female hormones that signal menstruation. Among anorectics, hypothalamic function is often abnormal. But the cause-and-effect sequence is still unclear.

Apert's syndrome   An inherited BIRTH DEFECT caused by a single gene, Apert's syndrome is more common among children born to older fathers. The signs include a peaked ("pointed") head caused by the premature closing of the different bone plates that make up the skull, and fused ("webbed") fingers and/or toes.

appendicitis   Until 1886, when appendicitis was first identified as a condition that could be treated by surgery, people with an infected appendix almost always died from peritonitis when the appendix "burst." Once appendectomy became common, deaths from appendicitis began to fall. They rose again after 1902 when doctors, learning that appendicitis was an infection, began prescribing laxatives to ease the constipation thought to cause the problem. In the 1930s, when laxative treatment was abandoned, the death rate once again fell. Today, there are 250,000 appendectomies and 15,000 to 20,000 deaths from appendicitis recorded every year.

Currently, the overall lifetime risk of appendicitis is one in 15. It is most common among people age 10 to 30, relatively rare among the very young and the very old. As for gender, the incidence is similar among males and females except for an epidemiologically peculiar period between puberty and age 25 to 30 when—for unexplained reasons—the ratio is three males to every two females.

arm How swiftly a ball is thrown depends on the length of the pitcher's forearm (the part of the arm from elbow to wrist) and the strength in the SHOULDERS. The longer the forearm and the stronger the shoulder, the faster the ball will travel.

Right from birth, the male forearm is generally longer than the female forearm. At PUBERTY, males gain a second advantage when a flood of testosterone broadens male shoulder bones and thickens male chest and shoulder muscles. As a result of this hormone-related growth, a man's upper body may be as much as two to three times more powerful than a woman's. That is why female athletes are unlikely to match the records set by men in sports such as discus throwing. When the baseball team needs a pitcher to throw the ball hard and fast across home plate, anatomy, not sexism, dictates that the best choice is a man.

arthritis Arthritis is an autoimmune disorder—a condition in which the body attacks its own tissues. Its cause is still unknown, but many experts agree with Rockefeller University rheumatologist Robert G. Lahita, who says that the female immune system is "so finely tuned that it has a greater opportunity to go awry, and it usually does."

According to the Arthritis Foundation, women comprise two-thirds of the more than 37 million Americans with arthritis, a gender difference first recognized more than 2,500 years ago by the great Greek physician Hippocrates of Cos.

Two forms of arthritis, GOUT and ANKYLOSING SPONDYLITIS, are about nine times more common among men. But osteoarthritis, the most common form of arthritis, affects twice as many women as men; rheumatoid arthritis is three times more common among women; and the ratio of women to men with SYSTEMIC LUPUS ERYTHEMATOSUS, also known as lupus, is four to one.

There is an apparent link between the SEX HORMONES, specifically estrogen, and some forms of arthritis. But the mechanism has not yet been identified and the effects may be maddeningly paradoxical. For example, women with rheumatoid arthritis who become pregnant (and consequently produce larger amounts of the sex hormones estrogen and progesterone) improve. Recently, doctors at the Fred Hutchinson Cancer Research Centers in Seattle have found that while a woman with rheumatoid arthritis is pregnant, her symptoms are relieved as steadily as though she were taking steroid drugs. (The symptoms do, however, return a few weeks after delivery.) On the other hand, the symptoms of lupus worsen during pregnancy, suggesting that the same hormones that relieve rheumatoid arthritis produce painful lupus "flares."

asthma   Asthma is a respiratory disorder characterized by narrowing of the air passages after exposure to a variety of unpleasant triggers including (but not limited to) air pollutants, allergens, drugs, exercise, variations in air temperature, and physical or emotional stress.

In the United States, as many as 10 percent of all children and 5 percent of all adults are asthmatic. Before PUBERTY, the ratio of boys to girls is approximately two to one. After that, the difference gradually disappears. After age 30, the number of people with asthma is pretty much evenly divided between men and women.

athlete's foot   Athlete's foot is the most common fungal infection to affect human beings—itchy, scaling lesions between the toes. It occurs most often among boys who have not yet reached PUBERTY. Among adults, it shows up about six times more frequently among men than among women, but this disproportion is almost certainly due to culture rather than biology. As a rule, women are much less likely than men to wander barefoot through locker rooms or to live in places like military barracks where they bathe together and could pass the athlete's foot fungus from one person to another. Even when they do frequent locker rooms or live in barracks, women athletes and military personnel seem to be more careful about drying their feet and toes thoroughly after bathing, while men are more likely just to blot their feet and stick them, damp, into socks and shoes, providing the perfect environment for the athlete's foot fungus to flourish.

B

back   Because of bulkier shoulder MUSCLES and broader shoulder bones, the male back is stronger than the female back—but equally vulnerable to pain. Back spasms appear to attack men and women alike. On the other hand, after exercise, when stress strikes, or on a warm day, the male back is more apt to be damp and sweaty due to gender-related PERSPIRATION patterns. Men perspire more heavily on the back and shoulders; women, under the arms.

baldness   When Aristotle said, "No boy ever gets bald, no woman and no castrated man," he was almost right. As they grow older, both men and women experience a natural thinning of the hair that may occasionally progress to baldness in spots. But men are far more susceptible to "male pattern bald-ness"—hair loss at the front and the top of the head starting early in life, sometimes while a man is in his early 20s.

Male pattern baldness is an X-LINKED TRAIT transmitted via a gene on the X chromosome. One-third of all men and women inherit the trait, but how strongly it manifests itself depends on a person's exposure to testosterone. The more testosterone, the more evident the hair loss. On average, half the sons and half the daughters of a man with male pattern baldness will inherit the trait, but under normal circumstances, it will be evident only in postadolescent boys and adult men. Women who inherit the male pattern baldness gene may begin to lose hair if they are exposed to an abnormally increased level of testosterone—for example, from a masculinizing tumor of the ovary.

The same situation prevails among the bald man's grandchildren. Half the children, whether born to the bald man's sons or his daughters, will inherit the trait, but it is likely that only the boys will show its effects.

basal metabolism   Metabolism is the sum of the chemical processes that contribute to the creation or destruction of body tissues. The basal metabolism is the amount of heat (energy) produced when the body is fully at rest, performing only the most essential activities such as breathing, circulating blood, and secreting substances vital to life. The energy needed to maintain these functions is measured in CALORIES. Gender is a factor in determining how many calories an individual needs to maintain basal metabolism.

For men, the most important factor is BODY COMPOSITION. A man's body has proportionately more muscle; a woman's, more fat. This is true even if both weigh precisely the same. Because muscle is active tissue that uses more energy than fat tissue, the number of calories a man expends in maintaining body function when he is completely at rest—an amount of calories called the resting energy expenditure or REE—is about 10 percent higher than in a woman.

For women, the menstrual cycle is a significant contributor to variations in the calories required for the resting energy expenditure. At ovulation, women are likely to experience a natural craving for additional calories to account for the extra energy needed to release an egg. A study done at the USDA Energy and Protein Nutrition Laboratory in Beltsville, Maryland of female basal metabolisms during the three phases of the menstrual cycle has shown that women may burn as much as 5 percent to 7 percent more energy while sleeping on the nights between ovulation and the onset of menstrual bleeding than during and after menstruation. As a result, scientists investigating basal metabolism in women in the future may be required either to study all the women at the same point in their respective menstrual cycles or take the differences in basal metabolism into account when calculating energy requirements or expenditures.

DETERMINING THE REE (RESTING ENERGY EXPENDITURE)

Every body is different, but to approximate the REE, begin by dividing the body's weight in pounds by 2.2 to get the weight in kilograms. Then use the following equation to get the REE:

Women	18–30 yrs.	(14.7 x weight in kg) + 496
	30–60	(8.7 x weight in kg) + 829
	60+	(10.5 x weight in kg) + 596
Men	18–30	(15.3 x weight in kg) + 679
	30–60	(11.6 x weight in kg) + 879
	60+	(13.5 x weight in kg) + 487

Source: National Research Council, *Recommended Dietary Allowances*, 10th ed. (Washington, D.C.: Academy of Sciences, 1989).

beard   Facial hair is a male secondary sex characteristic that appears at PUBERTY in response to surging levels of the male sex hormone testosterone. Because the female sex hormone estrogen suppresses the growth of facial hair, a woman's face is usually smooth. The abnormal growth of hair that sometimes occurs on a female face and body, a condition called hirsutism, may be a symptom of one of several disorders characterized by increased testosterone secretion, such as polycystic ovary disease, a testosterone-secreting ovarian tumor, Cushing's syndrome, cancer of the adrenal glands, an adrenal gland enzyme defect, or a tumor on the central nervous system. In each case, the body produces more than a normal amount of testosterone, which is then converted in the skin to dihydrotestosterone, the form of testosterone that stimulates hair follicles, thus producing an unexpected hairiness.

In old age, as hormone levels decline, even though men still have more facial hair, a man's beard will thin and a woman may sprout hair on her chin and upper lip. For most women, the hair is clearly visible but still softer and more downy than a man's. However, among women from southern Europe and the Mediterranean area, the new facial hair may be dark and coarse.

bed-wetting   At age four, about one-third of all children experience nocturnal enuresis—wetting the bed during sleep. Two years later, the total drops to one in ten; at age 12, to fewer than one in 30.

Like other sleep disorders such as SLEEPWALKING, NIGHTMARES, and night terrors, bed-wetting is more common among boys. At all ages, the number of boys whose parents report their wetting the bed is anywhere from two to four times the number of girls.

In rare instances (1 percent to 2 percent of the cases), bed-wetting could be traced to a physical cause such as a urinary tract infection, but in most cases, its cause has remained a mystery. Some experts thought that the increased incidence in boys might be traceable to the fact that girls learn bladder control at an earlier age than boys. Others suggested emotional triggers; a few believed that the numbers simply did not reflect the true situation—that more boys seemed to be affected simply because more parents of boys reported bed-wetting to their doctors.

But everyone knew that bed-wetting sometimes ran in families. Now, there may be an explanation for why this is so. In 1995, a group of Danish scientists at the Institute of Medical Biochemistry in Copenhagen examined the gene patterns of members of 11 families with a history of children who continued to wet their beds at night after the age of seven. What the researchers discovered was a genetic flaw—a mutation on chromosome 13, present in all the people with bed-wetting problems but not in their drier relatives. If a genetic flaw does turn out to be the culprit, the next task will be to find out why it affects boys more often than girls.

birth, premature   The term "premature" was originally defined by weight; a "premature baby" was any child who arrived weighing less than 2.5 kg (5.5 lb.). This is no longer regarded as appropriate because some small infants have spent a full nine months in development in the womb. They are simply small (but healthy) babies.

Today, the only babies considered truly premature are those born before the end of the normal nine-month gestation period. As a rule, boys are more likely to be born early; girls are more likely to be born late. Premature boys are more likely than premature girls to experience developmental problems such as respiratory distress [see LUNGS].

birth defects   Every year, approximately 250,000 babies are born with birth defects in the United States. Birth defects are the third leading cause of death in children younger than 14.

Some birth defects occur more commonly in one sex or the other. For example, girls are more likely than boys to be born with a dislocated HIP, while boys are more susceptible to congenital defects of the HEART, and, if they have a cleft lip or CLEFT PALATE, to have a more serious malformation. Boys are also at higher risk of X-LINKED TRAITS, defects transmitted via one or more genes on the X chromosome. These include (but are not limited to) COLOR BLINDNESS, Fabry's disease, FRAGILE X SYNDROME, HEMOPHILIA, ICTHYOSIS, and MUSCU-LAR DYSTROPHY.

As they grow older, both men and women are more likely to have children with birth defects. Because sperm and egg develop in different ways [see GERM CELLS], older women are at increased risk of transmitting defects due to the presence or absence of an entire chromosome, while older fathers are more likely to transmit defects due to a single damaged gene.

According to Jan M. Friedman, professor and head of the department of medical genetics at the University of British Columbia, single-gene defects such as ACHONDROPLASIA (a form of dwarfism), APERT'S SYNDROME (a pointed head and fusion of fingers into a single mass), and MARFAN'S SYNDROME (skeletal and vascular defects) are five times more common among babies whose fathers are older than 40 regardless of the mother's age. This is similar to the increased incidence of DOWN'S SYNDROME among babies born to 35-to-40-year-old mothers.

birth weight   In the United States, the average newborn weighs about 7.4 pounds. Because of their bulkier MUSCLE and heavier BONES, boys generally arrive weighing slightly more, about 7.5 pounds, while girls usually weigh slightly less, about an even 7 pounds.

Although environmental factors such as a pregnant woman's diet play an important role in determining a newborn baby's weight, there are important genetic influences at work as well. Male fetuses generally grow more rapidly than females; the accelerated growth is thought to be related to the muscle- and bone-building male sex hormone testosterone. As a general rule, however, a newborn human being's weight is equal to about 5 percent of its mother's weight.

bladder cancer   In the United States, a man's risk of bladder cancer is three times higher than a woman's. For 1994, the American Cancer Society estimated 51,200 new cases of bladder cancer—38,000 in men, 13,200 in women.

Some experts suggest that the difference is due to patterns of urination, with women urinating more frequently than men, thus emptying the bladder of irritants more quickly. The best-known risk factor for bladder cancer is smoking, which is still more common among men than among women. Tobacco smoke contains more than 4,000 chemical compounds, including at least 43 different known carcinogens such as benz-(a)-pyrene that may pass through the bladder on their way out of the body. It is clear that smoking is linked to nearly half the cases of bladder cancer in men and to about a third of the cases in women. Another important risk factor is exposure to industrial chemicals such as dyes, solvents, and the tanning agent used to process leather. Until now, jobs where these chemicals are present have been held primarily, if not exclusively, by men.

blindness   The leading causes of blindness in the United States are CATA-RACTS, DIABETES, and MACULAR DEGENERATION, all of which are more common among women than among men.

blood flow   In one study in the late 1980s, researchers at the Mayo Clinic in Rochester, Minnesota compared blood flow in the hands of healthy men and women with that of people with RAYNAUD'S DISEASE, a condition causing spasms in the small peripheral BLOOD VESSELS that lead to reduced blood flow to the tips of fingers, nose, and tongue. The study showed that even under normal conditions at room temperature, the flow of blood to a woman's hand is smaller than the flow of blood to a man's hand. Subsequent studies suggest that the female sympathetic nervous system—the nerves that control involuntary bodily functions such as heartbeat, breathing, and the dilation and constriction of blood vessels—exercises tighter control of blood flow.

The most interesting discovery was that the sympathetic nervous system is very amenable to manipulation. After a period of mental arithmetic or deep breathing or when the women's bodies were warmed one degree centigrade, blood flow to their hands not only equaled that of men, it surpassed it.

blood groups   A blood group (also known as a blood group system or blood type) is defined by the antigen (protein) a person carries on the surface of his or her RED BLOOD CELLS and the antibodies present in his or her blood serum. The antibodies act as agglutinins, substances that cause the specific blood cells to "agglutinate," that is, to clump together.

Currently, there are 22 known human blood groups. The best-known blood groups are A, B, AB, and O. People with type A blood have A antigens on their red blood cells and antibodies to blood type B in their blood serum. If they are given a transfusion of type B blood, the B antigens in the transfused blood will stimulate their type B antibodies to attack the type B cells, causing the cells to stick together and form potentially life-threatening blood clots. A similar reaction will occur if a person with type B blood (B antigens, A antibodies) is transfused with type A blood.

People with type AB blood have both A and B antigens, but no antibodies. They are "universal recipients" who can accept type A, type B, or type O blood. People with type O blood have neither A nor B antigens. They are "universal donors," but because they have both A and B antibodies, they can safely accept only O blood.

Blood type is an inherited trait. Forty-three percent of Americans are type O; 40 percent are type A; 10 percent, type B; 5 percent or fewer, type AB. The primary blood types occur equally among males and females. The only known sex-linked blood type is a subgroup called Xg. This subgroup was discovered in 1962 in the blood serum of a person who had undergone multiple transfusions. Xg blood type is an X-LINKED TRAIT, transmitted via a gene on the X chromosome. Like all X-linked traits, Xg blood occurs primarily in men.

Because blood type is inherited, it can be useful in settling disputed paternity cases. While having the same blood type as a child does not definitively identify a man as the father, having a blood type different from the child can eliminate him entirely. Blood groups are also useful in medical genetics, in drawing up a pedigree that shows how a genetic disease has been transmitted through several generations.

blood poisoning   Blood poisoning is the common name for a systemic infection more correctly known as septicemia (from the Greek words for blood and putrefaction). Septicemia is caused by microorganisms that release toxins that circulate through the blood vessels to every organ in the body.

For unknown reasons, septicemia appears to be more common among women. In 1991, it was the eighth leading cause of death among women in the United States, most commonly among women older than 75.

blood tests   Can a doctor really run a finger down a list of blood test results and say with some degree of certainty whether the person tested is male or female? It depends on what's being tested.

Gender has no known effect on the results of tests that measure blood sugar, or thyroid hormones, or how long it takes blood to clot, or the fragility of blood cells, or the number of WHITE BLOOD CELLS in a given sample of blood, or in blood tests for infectious diseases.

But in a number of other tests, the normal values may be significantly different for men and women. The classic example is hemoglobin, the pigment in RED BLOOD CELLS that carries oxygen throughout the body. Because men have proportionately more red blood cells, their hemoglobin levels are normally higher. So are their levels of ferritin, an IRON–protein complex carried in hemoglobin. The hematocrit, which measures the percentage of the blood sample that is composed of red blood cells, also naturally higher in men, is an indicator of how well the body is hydrated. A rising hematocrit indicates either an increase in red blood cells, which may be due to a blood disorder, or a decrease in the normal amount of fluids.

Clearly, the levels of SEX HORMONES vary by gender. While men and women both produce male and female hormones, a man's blood normally contains more testosterone, a woman's more estrogen. Androstenedione, a hormone similar to but less potent than testosterone, is secreted by the adrenal cortex (the capsule covering the adrenal gland) and converted by the liver to estrone, a form of estrogen. After menopause, when a woman's ovaries no longer secrete estrogen, the conversion of androstenedione provides a continuing, though reduced, supply of female hormone. Men normally have higher androstenedione levels; in either sex, a rise in androstenedione may suggest a tumor of the gonads (ovaries, testes) or the adrenal glands.

Human growth hormone is another hormone whose blood levels vary by gender, with male levels generally twice as high as female levels. Growth hormone readings are useful in evaluating dwarfism or in diagnosing a tumor of the pituitary gland or the hypothalamus. Levels of the thyroid hormone calcitonin are also higher in men. Calcitonin prevents the body from reabsorbing bone and thus may protect men from the drastic bone loss that women are likely to experience after menopause. Luteinizing hormone, secreted by the pituitary gland, causes ovulation in women and stimulates the production of testosterone in men. The normal male values are only 20 percent to 30 percent of the normal female values.

Gender is a factor in the blood levels for some enzymes. Gamma glutamyl transferase is an enzyme that reflects liver function, including the metabolism of ALCOHOL. The normal levels of gamma glutamyl transferase are higher for men than for women. Alkaline phosphatase is an enzyme in cell membranes. A sudden increase in alkaline phosphatase suggests bone damage, so alkaline phosphatase levels are used to monitor cancer patients and provide an early warning of any metastasis to the bones. Normally, a man has higher levels of alkaline phosphatase than a woman has.

BLOOD TESTS WITH GENDER-RELATED RESULTS

Substance	Male	Female (adult)	Female (postmenopause)
Blood cells			
Ferritin	20–300 ng/ml	20–120 ng/ml	
Hematocrit	42–54%	38–46%	
Hemoglobin	14–18 g/dl	12–16 g/dl	11.7–13.6 g/dl
Hormones			
Androstenedione	0.9–1.7 ng/ml	0.6–3 ng/ml	(0.3–8 ng/ml after menopause)
Calcitonin*	0.210–0.265 ng/ml	0.105–0.120 ng/ml	
Estrogen	12–34 pg/ml	24–186 pg/ml depending on menstrual cycle	
Human growth hormone	0–10 ng/dl	0–5 ng/dl	
Luteinizing hormone	5–20 mIU/ml	5–60 mIU/ml	50–100 mIU/ml
Testosterone	300–1,200 ng/dl	30–95 ng/dl	
Enzymes			
Alkaline phosphatase	90–239 units/L	76–196 units/L	87–250 units/L
Gamma glutamyl transferase	6–37 units/L	5–27 units/L	6–37 units/L

Source: *Diagnostic Tests Handbook*, ed. Regina Daley Ford (Springhouse, PA: Springhouse Corporation, 1986).

*Depending on test.

blood vessels   A woman's blood vessels are more flexible and expand more easily than a man's. One result of this is that premenopausal women are less likely than adult men of the same age to develop HIGH BLOOD PRESSURE or to suffer a heart attack triggered by a blockage of the coronary artery.

It is clear that female hormones play a major role in maintaining the elasticity of female blood vessels. A woman's blood vessels are most elastic during pregnancy, when estrogen and progesterone levels are high and the vessels must expand to accommodate as much as a 40 percent increase in blood volume for the growing fetus. Conversely, after menopause, when the ovaries no longer secrete estrogen, a woman's protective advantage against high blood pressure and heart disease diminishes. Past middle age, a woman's risk of coronary artery disease rises and, for the first time, the percentage of women with hypertension exceeds that of men.

blood volume   In general, the amount of blood in the human body is related to the body's size. Bigger people have more blood; so a man's body generally contains more blood than a woman's body. The exception occurs during pregnancy, when a woman's blood vessels stretch and the volume of blood in her body increases in greater amounts than can be accounted for simply by her increase in weight.

For some unexplained reason, there is a smaller increase in blood volume with a female fetus than with a male fetus. This may be one explanation for the finding by the government-funded, long-running Collaborative Perinatal Project that women carrying female fetuses gain less weight and are less likely to experience swelling in their hands and face.

body composition   Pound for pound, women have more body FAT; men, more MUSCLE. A woman's body is 20 percent to 25 percent stored fat; up to 35 percent of its weight is muscle tissue. A man's body is 15 percent to 20 percent fat; up to 42 percent of its weight is muscle.

These differences arise from the effects of the SEX HORMONES. Testosterone is an anabolic steroid that promotes the synthesis of proteins and the growth of tissue, specifically muscle. Estrogen is a catabolic steroid; it helps metabolize proteins and produces a larger supply of stored fat.

Muscle weighs more than fat and burns more calories (energy), so a man weighs more and can consume more calories than a woman of the same height and general build without gaining weight. There is more water in muscle than in fat, so a man's body contains proportionately more liquid. Men can drink more ALCOHOL without getting tipsy because the extra liquid in their bodies dilutes the alcohol, making it less potent.

body odor   Body odor is caused by bacteria that live on the skin and digest the milky secretions released by apocrine sweat glands—the sweat glands found under the arm, around the nipples, and in the groin.

A person's body odor, one of several million possible combinations of the approximately one dozen odorous acidic organic compounds found in underarm PERSPIRATION, is a characteristic as individual as a fingerprint.

In 1990, chemist George Preți of Philadelphia's famed Monelle Institute of Chemical Senses narrowed the potentially odorous compounds to those with six to eleven carbon atoms, the most important a hexanoic acid* with a methyl group** attached at one of the carbon atoms. Precursors of this compound are found in the water-soluble portion of the secretions from the apocrine sweat glands. Lewis Thomas, the author of the best-selling *Lives of a Cell*, wrote that what determines the combination may be the same molecule that creates the major histocompatibility complex that distinguishes one person immunologically from another and makes our tissues incompatible.

Because apocrine sweat glands do not develop fully until an individual reaches puberty, their secretions and the resulting odor are thought to be a device for attracting the opposite sex. In other words, body odor may work like sexual pheromones, the chemical attractants emitted by animals. In a recent study, researchers at the University of Chicago discovered that among Hutterites, a sect of Anabaptists living in parts of Canada and the American northwest, men and women instinctively choose partners whose histocompatibility is most different from theirs, a device that ensures the greatest possible variation in gene patterns among their children in a closed society.

Deodorants are cosmetics that contain antibacterial agents to kill the bacteria that make malodorous chemicals, plus fragrance to mask the odor. Antiperspirants add aluminum salts that make pores swell and inhibit the formation and release of sweat. Apocrine sweating decreases naturally in old age, particularly among females; the elderly rarely require deodorants.

body shape   As a rule, women store fat tissue at BREAST and HIP; men, at SHOULDERS and abdomen. This, along with male/female differences in MUSCLE and BONE structure, produces two distinct body types sometimes picturesquely described as "apples" (fat around the middle) and "pears" (fat around the hips).

---

* a compound with eight carbon atoms
**a molecule with one carbon and three hydrogen atoms

Forty years ago, scientists first noted the protective effect of fat around the hips when they discovered that women who are fat around the waist like a typically apple-shaped male seem more likely than pear-shaped women to develop diabetes and atherosclerosis (coronary artery disease). By the 1980s, science had begun to link upper body fat (the apple) to an increased risk of heart disease and diabetes in both men and women.

At the American Heart Association's 15th science writers' forum in New Orleans in January 1988, researchers from Rockefeller University in New York proposed a mechanism that might account for the apple versus pear shapes. All fat cells, they said, have two distinct hormone-binding structures on their surface, alpha receptors and beta receptors. Both types of receptors bind the hormones epinephrine and norepinephrine, but the relative number of alpha or beta receptors activated during the binding process appears to influence the distribution of body fat. Activated beta cells stimulate the production of an enzyme inside the fat cell that keeps the cell from accumulating fat; activated alpha cells inhibit the production of this enzyme, allowing the fat cell to grow bigger.

In both sexes, alpha receptor activity is higher in the buttocks. In men, alpha receptor activity is higher in the abdomen. In women, alpha activity is normally high in the hips and thighs; among women who are breast-feeding, however, alpha activity in these traditional areas is temporarily reduced, making fat available elsewhere in the body, i.e. to the breast, where it serves as an energy depot for the nursing mother.

There are economic as well as scientific aspects to male/female differences in body shapes. Men's bodies, while they may be taller or shorter than the arbitrary average ("regular") size, generally conform to a wedge shape that can be accommodated by changing the size of the clothing at the chest and altering the length from shoulder to seat to produce "short," "tall," and "extra tall" apparel with pretty much the same relative proportions. Women's clothes must take into account a dizzying variety of bust and hip sizes as well as the relative differences in distance between bust and waist. Because there are more variables to the female body shape, there are more women's apparel sizes.

bones   Like all body tissues, bone is constantly being renewed as old bone cells are resorbed (broken down and assimilated by the body) and replaced with new ones. Cells called osteoclasts create small cavities in bones, and other cells, called osteoblasts, refill the spaces with new bone, a process governed by human growth hormone and influenced by the sex hormones estrogen and testosterone.

Estrogen prevents the excess resorption of bone tissue; testosterone stimulates the growth of stronger, more dense bone tissue.

Even in young adulthood, when bones are strongest and most dense, the average woman has 30 percent less bone mass than the average man. As they age, both men and women lose bone density, but women lose more and they lose it faster. A woman may lose as much as 2 percent of her bone mass each year in the first five years after menopause. After that, her bone loss slows to about 1 percent a year. Over her entire lifetime, she may lose 50 percent of her trabecular (spongy) bone in vertebrae and at the rounded ends of the long bones, and 35 percent of her cortical bone, the denser bone tissue in long bones such as the femur. A man, however, will lose only 25 percent of both trabecular and cortical bone.

This gender-related difference is generally attributed to the steeper, more dramatic decline in a postmenopausal woman's secretion of bone-protecting estrogen. The visible result is a higher incidence of OSTEOPOROSIS and a higher rate of fractures among older women as compared with older men. Currently, the incidence of age-related osteoporosis is six times higher among women.

brain   The average adult human brain weighs about three pounds, and, in the words of British writer Anthony Smith, author of *The Body*, is "so full of water that it tends to slump like a blancmange if placed without support on a firm surface."

As a rule, a male brain is about 10 percent heavier than a female brain, reflecting a general difference in body size. The heaviest human brain ever recorded, weighing 5 pounds 1.1 ounces at autopsy at the University of Chicago in December 1992, had belonged to a 30-year-old male. The lighest normal (not atrophied or mummified) brain on record had belonged to a 31-year-old woman. It weighed 2 pounds 6.7 ounces on the scales at King's College Hospital in London in 1977.

Neuroscientists have identified a growing number of discrete gender-related differences in brain anatomy. In the male brain, the right hemisphere—which controls visual and SPATIAL REASONING—is noticeably larger and heavier than the right hemisphere of the female brain, while the female brain has more connections between the left and right hemispheres [see CORPUS CALLOSUM].

With age, the male brain seems to deteriorate at a faster clip. In April 1991, a team of researchers at the University of Pennsylvania used magnetic resonance imaging (MRI) to measure the relative atrophy of brain fluid and tissue in 34 men and 35 women aged 18 to 80. They found brain tissue in the male brains deteriorating two to three times faster than in female brains. In addition, the male brains showed more changes on the left side, the side that governs LANGUAGE AND SPEECH; changes in the women's brains were symmetric. There is continuing speculation that estrogen may retard the aging of brain cells and help preserve memory, but the results of research into the value of hormone replacement for older women with ALZHEIMER'S DISEASE are ambivalent.

brain cells   There are approximately 10 billion neurons (nerve cells) in a human brain, but the female brain generally has about 11 percent more brain cells than the male, according to Sandra Witelson of McMaster University (Canada), who painstakingly counted the cells in five male and four female brains after death. Witelson found the extra neurons packed into two of the six layers of the female cerebral cortex (the outer part of the brain) in an area right behind the eyes that is used for understanding language and recognizing melody, including the melody implicit in the tones of human speech. (For more on Witelson's brain research, see CORPUS CALLOSUM and LANGUAGE AND SPEECH.)

breast   Boys and girls begin life with similar breast tissue, but at puberty the breast becomes distinctly male or female. While both men and women experience a darkening of the nipples and areola (the circle of puckered flesh around the nipple), only women develop milk glands and a characteristic fatty tissue, changes stimulated by rising levels of the female sex hormone estrogen. At maturity, all women have similar amounts of glandular breast tissue. It is the difference in the amount of fatty tissue that accounts for the differences in female breast size.

Sometimes men do experience a growth of fatty breast tissue. This condition, known as gynecomastia, may be due to a hormonal imbalance, or to obesity, or to the influence of one of a number of medical drugs including, but not limited to, the antibiotic chlortetracycline (Aureomycin); the anticancer drugs busulfan (Myleran) and vincristine (Oncovin); the antidepressant phenelzine (Nardil), and tricyclic antidepressants such as amytriptilline (Elavil); the antiemetic metaclopramide (Reglan); the antifungal griseofulvin (Fulvicin) [when taken by mouth]; the antihypertensives clonidine (Catapres) and methyldopa (Aldomet); the diuretic spironolactone (Aldactone); the female hormones estrogen and DES, as well as the male hormone testosterone, which can be converted to estrogen in the body; the tranquilizers chlorpromazine (Thorazine), haloperidol (Haldol), reserpine, and thioridazine (Mellaril, etc.); the tuberculosis drugs ethionamide (Trecator-SC) and isoniazid (INH, Nydrazind); and the ulcer drug cimetadine (Tagamet). These drugs may also cause breast enlargement in women.

breast cancer   Breast cancer is predominantly, but not exclusively, a female disease. In 1994, the American Cancer Society estimated 182,000 new cases of breast cancer (1,000 among men) and 49,000 deaths (300 among men).

Although breast cancer is much less common in men, it is as dangerous as breast cancer in women. The risk factors for men are similar to those for women: a family history of the disease, exposure to estrogen, and exposure to ionizing radiation. Men who develop breast cancer tend to be diagnosed at around age 60, later than the average age for women, and the prognosis for male breast cancer patients, even those diagnosed apparently early in the disease, is more pessimistic than for women. At diagnosis, the five-year survival rate for women with Stage I breast cancer (a lump ¾ inch or smaller with no spread to lymph nodes) is 85 percent; for men, it is 50 percent. Nearly 66 percent of the women with Stage II disease (palpable nodes and a tumor one to two inches in diameter) will be alive five years after diagnosis; only 33 percent of the men with similar tumors will survive that long. While recurrences are relatively rare (about 2 percent), some physicians advocate preventive removal of the other breast among men who are extremely fearful or who have a strong family history of breast cancer.

bruises   The most common vascular disorder is an increased fragility of the small blood vessels just under the skin that leads to easy bruising. Patients often complain of bruises that develop spontaneously on thighs, buttocks, and upper arms. There is usually no apparent reason for the problem, and in the absence of a blood disease such as leukemia, blood tests are normal and the patient generally has no other abnormal bleeding episodes, although there may be a family history of easy bruising. For unknown reasons, this condition is more common among women.

bulimia   Bulimia is an EATING DISORDER characterized by repeated sessions of binge eating during which a person may consume anywhere from 1,000 to 50,000 calories at one sitting. Like ANOREXIA NERVOSA, bulimia is more common among women than among men. Overall, as many as 4 percent of all young adult women in the United States are bulimic; the incidence of true bulimia among college women, the group at highest risk, is estimated to be slightly less than 2 percent.

There may be a link between hormones and bulimia. In 1988, researchers Thomas D. Geracioti, Jr. of the National Institutes of Health and Roger A. Liddle of Duke University in Durham, North Carolina found that women suffering from bulimia appear to secrete lower-than-normal amounts of a hormone known as cholecystokin (CCK).

CCK is produced by glands in the small intestine. It is secreted in response to eating and plays an important role in determining satiety (the feeling of fullness after meals). Among the bulimics in this study, CCK levels after eating were only half as high as the CCK levels for people who were not bulimic. The women with bulimia also reported feeling less full after eating; those who were given antidepressants for eight weeks showed normal CCK responses after eating. The researchers were unable to explain the effects of antidepressants on CCK levels.

bunions   A bunion is a localized swelling of the metatarsophalangeal joint, the place where the big toe (also known as "hallux") joins the foot. In adolescence, girls sometimes develop a deformity in which the big toe bends outward and a bunion forms over the joint. Bunions are painful only when a person is wearing shoes, and the discomfort can almost always be relieved by wearing shoes that are wide enough not to press on the deformed joint.

C

calcium   Male or female, the adult human body contains about 1,200 grams (40 ounces/2.5 pounds) of calcium. Ninety-nine percent of this calcium is in the bones; the rest is found in the teeth, in the fluids between cells, in the cell membranes, and in structures such as the cell nucleus.

Calcium is essential to life. It enables nerve cells to transmit impulses, makes it possible for MUSCLE fibers to contract and blood to clot, facilitates the passage of various substances including nutrients through cell membranes, and may even prevent the buildup of fatty deposits of CHOLESTEROL in the arteries. Hormones, including the SEX HORMONES, maintain the body's calcium level and ensure a constant flow of calcium to the various organs. If a person does not consume

RECOMMENDED CALCIUM CONSUMPTION		
Gender/Age	NIH (mg/day)	RDA (mg/day)
Women		
25–49 yrs.	1,000	800
pregnant/nursing	1,200–1,500	1,200
50–64 yrs.		
taking estrogen	1,000	800
not taking estrogen	1,500	800
65+ yrs.	1,500	800
Men		
25–64 yrs.	1,000	800
65+ yrs.	1,500	800

Source: National Institutes of Health Consensus Development Panel on Optimal Calcium Intake, June 1994. *Recommended Dietary Allowances*, 10th ed. (Washington, D.C.: National Academy Press, 1989).

GOOD SOURCES OF CALCIUM

Food Portions That Provide 100–200 mg Calcium

Broccoli, cooked	½ cup
Cheese (blue, brick, camembert, cheddar, feta, gouda, Monterey, mozzarella, muenster, provolone, roquefort, swiss)	1 ounce
Cheese, ricotta	¼ cup
English muffin	1
Milk, whole	½ cup
Milk, lowfat	½ cup
Salmon, canned, drained (with bones)	3 ounces
Spinach, cooked	½ cup
Tofu	¼ cup
Yogurt, plain, whole milk	4 ounces
Yogurt, plain, lowfat	2 ounces

Note: These quantities are provided for comparison. It is worth noting that one cup of milk provides up to half the entire requirement for a healthy adult.

Source: *Good Sources of Nutrients* (Washington, D.C.: USDA, Human Nutrition Services, January 1990).

---

enough calcium in food or supplements, the body will compensate by pulling calcium from the bones so as to supply the cells and sustain the basic life functions.

Early in life, the body absorbs calcium and builds strong bones fairly easily, reaching a peak density sometime between age 20 and 35. In an effort to increase calcium absorption and bone growth among young people so as to provide a measure of insurance in old age, when less calcium is absorbed and the bones become more porous, the National Institutes of Health has suggested raising the daily consumption of calcium. These new levels have not yet been accepted by the National Research Council, which issues the recommended dietary allowances (RDA).

calories   A calorie is a unit of energy—the amount of energy required to raise the temperature of one gram of water by one degree centigrade. Dieters and biochemists measure the units of potential energy from food in terms of calories. For example, a three-ounce portion of skinless, boneless white meat chicken provides 100 calories of potential energy to the body.

How many calories an individual requires depends on several factors, including gender, body size, age, and level of activity (energy expenditure). The amount of energy it takes to run the body when it is totally at rest is called the BASAL METABOLISM or the resting energy expenditure (REE).

A person's total calorie/energy requirement for the day is the REE plus a sufficient amount of calories to provide energy for the body's "work"—thinking, speaking, studying, walking, running, driving, typing, chasing the baby, cooking, and so forth. A man's REE is about 10 percent higher than a woman's. This makes it possible for him to hold his weight steady while consuming 10 percent more calories than a woman of the same age and weight who performs the same amount of physical work.

No woman can acquire this masculine advantage by dieting to get rid of her body fat. No matter how stringently she diets, her body will never have the same ratio of fat to muscle that is found in the body of an adult man. You can see this for yourself just by calling up the image of two adults, one male, one female, each 5'8" tall, each weighing 120 pounds, both doing the same amount of work each day. The thin woman still has minimal curves, but the skinny man does not. He is all skin and bones, more muscle than fat, and he will still burn more calories than she will.

For example, an average 25-year-old, 120-pound woman's REE is 1,297 calories a day. A 25-year-old, 120-pound man's is 1,518 calories. A 17-year-old 120-pound boy's is 1,606 calories. To figure out how many calories they each need each day, you have to know how much work they do, but if all three do the same amount of work, and the thin woman and the skinny man eat as much as the boy, both adults will gain weight. The woman will gain more because her REE requires fewer calories.

CALORIE REQUIREMENTS: MEN VERSUS WOMEN

To find out how many calories a person can consume each day without gaining weight, multiply the REE [see BASAL METABOLISM] by the appropriate "activity factor" below:

Light activity	Men	1.6
(housecleaning, child care,	Women	1.5
golf, sailing, table tennis)		
Moderate activity	Men	1.7
(cycling, skiing, tennis)	Women	1.6
Heavy activity	Men	2.1
(heavy digging, mountain	Women	1.9
climbing, football)		

Source: National Research Council, *Recommended Dietary Allowances*, 10th ed. (National Academy Press, 1989).

Worse yet, going on a diet may actually lower the number of calories she can consume and still hold her weight. "What you call dieting, your body calls starvation, and consequently slows its metabolism in order to conserve energy," says Joan Gussow, professor of nutrition and education at Teachers College, Columbia University in New York. Slower metabolism equals fewer calories burned equals more pounds gained (or retained) *in the consumption of the same amount of food.*

cancer   Cancer is the second leading cause of death in the United States, second only to heart disease. Although some cancers, such as cancer of the breast, are more common among women, overall, fewer women than men develop cancer and fewer women than men die of the disease. A man's risk of

REPORTED DEATHS FROM CANCER, 1991

Age	Male	Female
All ages (yrs.)	272,380	242,277
1–14	938	694
15–34	3,699	3,434
35–54	27,529	29,302
55–74	142,089	111,419
75+	98,067	97,388

Source: National Center for Health Statistics, *Vital Statistics of the United States, 1991* (Washington, D.C.: Public Health Service, 1994).

ESTIMATED DEATHS FROM CANCER, 1992

Age	Male	Female
Less than 1 yr.	40	20
1–14	910	610
15–24	1,070	570
25–34	2,610	2,640
35–44	8,080	9,480
45–54	20,290	20,450
55–64	50,910	41,510
65–74	90,750	69,900
75–84	76,780	66,810
85+	24,720	32,900

Source: U.S. Centers for Disease Control, "Provisional numbers of deaths for the 10 leading causes of death by age, race and sex, United States, 1992," *Monthly Vital Statistics*, September 28, 1993.

developing some form of cancer over the course of his entire lifetime; is 1-in-2; a woman's, 1-in-3.

This difference may be due in part to genetic influences, but there is also an environmental component at work. More men than women smoke; more men than women are exposed to potential carcinogens in the workplace. Until an equal number of men and women are exposed to these risks, it will be impossible to determine with any certainty the true impact of gender on the overall risk of cancer.

canker sores   Canker sores (also known as aphthous ulcers) are common, recurrent, painful lesions on the mucous membrane lining the cheek. Canker sores are not herpes infections, but they are likely to pop up after a herpes infection elsewhere in the mouth or body. Some follow an injury to the tissue. For others, the cause remains a mystery. For some as-yet-unknown reason, they are more common among women.

carpal tunnel syndrome   Carpal tunnel syndrome is an intensely painful condition of the wrist and hand resulting from compression of the median nerve located in the "tunnel" created by the carpal bones and ligaments in the wrist. The nerve controls some movements of the thumb, index finger, middle finger, and half of the ring finger.

Carpal tunnel syndrome is two to five times more common among women, especially women in their 40s, 50s, and 60s. It typically follows repetitive work such as typing, writing, drawing, knitting, needlepoint, or working with tools, but it is also linked to an underactive thyroid gland, diabetes, a fracture, an infection, or acromegaly, a disorder of the pituitary gland. Carpal tunnel syndrome also occurs more frequently among pregnant women and in women using birth control pills, perhaps because both pregnancy and oral contraceptives cause an accumulation of fluid in the hands.

cataract   A cataract is a clouding of the lens of the eye, a condition more common in women than in men. Cataracts blur vision and, if left untreated, may lead to blindness. Today, cataracts are responsible for 9 percent of blindness in the United States. Cataracts are generally age-related, but may also be linked to diabetes, high blood pressure, use of steroid drugs, exposure to electromagnetic radiation, and nearsightedness.

chocolate   When a man is serious about pleasing a woman, he comes courting with a box of chocolates. It's a smart move. The anecdotal female preference for chocolate has scientific underpinnings based on nutritional chemistry and gender-related FOOD CRAVINGS.

Chocolate is rich in stimulants, containing not only caffeine (a central nervous system stimulant) but also theobromine (a muscle stimulant found primarily in tea leaves) and theophylline (a heart muscle stimulant, smooth muscle relaxant, diuretic, and blood vessel dilator used to treat bronchial ASTHMA and other forms of CHRONIC OBSTRUCTIVE PULMONARY DISEASE [COPD]).

Perhaps equally important, chocolate is a good source of fat. Despite its current bad press, fat is an important nutrient, a constituent of every cell membrane and of myelin, the sheath that covers nerve fibers that transmit impulses from cell to cell. Fat is also our most concentrated source of food energy (calories). It provides nine calories per gram, more than twice the four calories per gram we get from protein or carbohydrates.

Given a free choice, both men and women instinctively opt for foods rich in fat. But studies of food preferences suggest that women are more likely to pick high fat sweets, while men choose high fat protein. In other words, the quintessential "male" fatty food is a hamburger with fries; the perfect "female" indulgence, chocolate.*

cholesterol   Before puberty, during adolescence, and after menopause, more girls and women have total serum cholesterol levels at the higher end of the scale. Only during the reproductive years, from age 20 through 50, are men more likely than women to have high cholesterol levels. At all ages until menopause, women also have higher levels of high density LIPOPROTEINS, the "good" particles that carry cholesterol and fats out of the body rather than into arteries.

While most of the worry about cholesterol concerns its effects on the heart, specifically the higher incidence of heart attacks among young adult and middle-aged men and the increased incidence of heart attacks among post-menopausal women, it is worth noting that high cholesterol levels may also interfere with male sexual performance. The same high fat, high cholesterol diet that may lead to blockage of the coronary arteries and increase the risk of a heart

---

* When the Spanish brought chocolate back to Europe from Mexico, they drank it in secret in monasteries. It took a woman, Anne of Austria, to make chocolate an openly enjoyed delight. Having tasted chocolate at home, Anne took it with her to the court of France when she married Louis XIII. Spain's Maria Theresa appointed a royal chocolate-maker when she married Louis XIV. Madame Du Barry gave it a final boost into general popularity when she handed it around as a guaranteed aphrodisiac, a characteristic that depended less on chocolate's stimulants than on the pepper then added as a spice. Pepper oils, excreted through the bladder, irritated sensitive membranes to produce a sensation some mistook for amorous stirrings. *C'est la vie.*

attack may also block penile blood flow, says Dr. Arthur I. Burnett, a urologist in the male sexual dysfunction clinic at Johns Hopkins Medical Centers in Baltimore, Maryland. A reduction in blood flow to the penis caused by a blockage in arteries in the leg or penis itself would "certainly" affect a man's ability to sustain an erection, he says.

While there are any number of rigorous diets and regimens designed to lower cholesterol, a 1993 study from the University of Texas Southwestern Medical Center in Dallas suggests a simple, more palatable solution: CALCIUM. In this study, men given calcium supplements for ten days showed an average 13 percent drop in cholesterol levels.

PERCENTAGE OF ADULTS WITH TOTAL SERUM CHOLESTEROL OF 170 MG/DL OR MORE

Age (yrs.)	Cholesterol (total)	Race	Male	Female
0–9	170 mg/dl	white	29%	33%
	or higher	black	40	50
10–19	170 mg/dl	white	25	29
	or higher	black	34	41
20–29	200 mg/dl	white	23	27
	or higher	black	32	32
	240 mg/dl	white	5	7
	or higher	black	10	8
30–39	200 mg/dl	white	54	34
	or higher	black	41	37
	240 mg/dl	white	18	10
	or higher	black	9	7
40–49	200 mg/dl	white	60	53
	or higher	black	60	50
	240 mg/dl	white	21	18
	or higher	black	17	18
50–59	200 mg/dl	white	73	74
	or higher	black	60	76
	240 mg/dl	white	32	36
	or higher	black	24	36
60+	200 mg/dl	white	65	78
	or higher	black	59	78
	240 mg/dl	white	26	41
	or higher	black	30	41

Source: American Heart Association *Heart and Stroke Facts, 1994 supplement* (Dallas: American Heart Association, 1994).

REPORTED DEATHS FROM COPD, 1991

Age	Male	Female
All ages (yrs.)	50,485	40,165
1–14	109	*
15–34	*	*
35–54	*	1,502
55–74	21,944	17,049
75+	25,579	21,272

*COPD does not rank among the top ten causes of death in this age group.

Source: National Center for Health Statistics, *Vital Statistics of the United States, 1991* (Washington, D.C.: Public Health Service, 1994).

chronic obstructive pulmonary disease (COPD)   Chronic obstructive pulmonary diseases, including emphysema, are the fifth leading cause of death in the United States. Like lung cancer, COPD has always been more common among men than among women, almost certainly because men are more likely than women to smoke and to work with lung-damaging chemicals. As the number of women smokers rises and as women move into chemical and manufacturing jobs previously monopolized by men, the likely prospect is that their risk of COPD will rise to equal that of men.

cirrhosis of the liver   Cirrhosis of the liver is a progressive disease that destroys liver cells. In 1991, it was the sixth leading cause of reported deaths

ESTIMATED DEATHS FROM COPD, 1992

Age	Male	Female
Less than 1 yr.	40	—
1–14	110	80
15–24	80	110
25–34	160	90
35–44	490	300
45–54	1,280	1,140
55–64	5,580	4,510
65–74	16,130	12,690
75–84	19,420	14,760
85+	7,410	7,040

Source: U.S. Centers for Disease Control, "Provisional numbers of deaths for the 10 leading causes of death by age, race and sex, United States, 1992," *Montly Vital Statistics*, September 28, 1993.

among Americans age 35 to 54, and the seventh leading cause among those age 55 to 74.

Cirrhosis may result from several diseases, conditions, and life-style choices such as heart disease, a tumor that blocks the bile duct, malnutrition, and ALCOHOL abuse, also a risk factor for LIVER CANCER. On average, women seem to develop alcohol-induced cirrhosis at levels of consumption lower than those required to cause damage in the male liver, perhaps because women produce smaller amounts of the enzymes needed to digest alcohol and cannot metabolize alcohol as quickly and efficiently as men.

That being true, it's logical to assume that the higher male incidence of liver cancer and cirrhosis of the liver arises from the fact that more men drink to excess. If an equal number of men and women consumed excessive amounts of alcohol, we might expect to see a turnaround in the gender ratio for both diseases.

AGE GROUPS IN WHICH CIRRHOSIS OF THE LIVER IS AMONG 10 LEADING CAUSES OF DEATH, 1991

Age	Male	Female
35–54 yrs.	5,767	2,274
55–74	7,827	4,442

Source: National Center for Health Statistics, *Vital Statistics of the United States, 1991* (Washington, D.C.: Public Health Service, 1994).

cleft palate   In the United States, one of every 1,000 newborns has a cleft lip or palate resulting from the failure of the embryo's facial folds to come together smoothly. The defect does not seem to be linked to a specific gene. It occurs equally often in boys and girls, but boys with a cleft lip or palate are likely to have a more severe deformity, while women seem to be more likely to pass the defect on to their children. Cleft palate is one of the traits associated with fetal alcohol syndrome (FAS).

cold, tolerance for   Because of gender-related differences in BODY COMPOSITION, IRON storage, and BLOOD VESSELS, women react more acutely to cold TEMPERATURES.

Women have more FAT, men more MUSCLE. Muscle is "active" tissue. It converts more energy and generates more internal heat than fat does; a man's BASAL METABOLISM is higher than a woman's. Fat is "passive" tissue. It is a storehouse for energy and an excellent insulator for the internal organs; but this insulation keeps the heat produced in the body's core from reaching the skin, where cold is perceived. Put a man and a woman in the same room with the same middling-cool temperature, and the woman will feel cold first and stay chilled longer.

A chilled body attempts to warm itself with involuntary muscle contractions ("shivers") that help convert stored energy into body heat. The enzymes that facilitate the reaction are iron-dependent. Iron is carried around the body in RED BLOOD CELLS. Women have fewer red blood cells and lower stores of iron. Therefore, they have a more difficult time generating the shivering reaction needed to warm a cold body.

According to Henry C. Lukaski, research physiologist at the U.S. Department of Agriculture Human Nutrition Research Center in Grand Forks, North Dakota, women of childbearing age who are even modestly iron-deficient cannot use the energy stored in their bodies to warm themselves. To prove his thesis, Lukaski put six healthy women volunteers on a low-iron diet for 80 days, then tested them to see how well they could tolerate cold. Then he put them on an iron-rich regimen for 100 days to raise their body reserves of iron and retested them for cold tolerance. On the low-iron diet, the volunteers started shivering after 84 minutes in a room where a cool draft was blowing. On the high-iron diet, they were able to stay in the cold room for an additional eight minutes without shivering, and their bodies stayed warmer throughout the entire test.

Finally, a woman's body is more likely to react strongly to cold because women are more likely to have RAYNAUD'S DISEASE. Raynaud's, which runs in families and is most common among women aged 20 to 50, exacerbates the reaction to cold. People with Raynaud's already have reduced circulation of blood to the extremities due to a thickening of the inner wall of the blood vessels. When the vessels shut tighter in response to cold, most or all of the blood supply to the fingertips and toes may be blocked, says rheumatologist Carolyn Bell of the University of Wisconsin–Madison Center for Health Sciences. These symptoms are worst in the winter months, but they can also be triggered by air conditioning, immersion in cold water, or even by reaching into the refrigerator/freezer.

color blindness   Total color blindness, a complete inability to distinguish colors other than shades of black, gray, and white, is a rare disorder caused by a recessive gene carried on an autosomal chromosome (a chromosome other than the X or Y chromosome). This defect, which occurs equally in men and women, only shows up in people who inherit a defective gene from both parents. If they inherit only one copy of the defective gene, it will not produce the defect.

Partial color blindness, such as an inability to distinguish between red and green, is another story. It, too, is caused by a recessive gene, but this gene is "X-LINKED," carried on the X chromosome. Women have two X chromosomes; men, one X chromosome and one Y chromosome. Therefore, a woman who gets one X chromosome with the gene for red–green color blindness can counter it with her other X chromosome, but a man whose only X chromosome carries the defective gene will be red–green color-blind. Consequently, this defect is far more common among men than among women.

The greater male susceptibility continues into future generations. If a color-blind woman with two X chromosomes carrying the red–green color vision defect marries a color-blind man, all their offspring will be color-blind. If a color-blind man marries a woman with normal color vision, their sons will have normal color vision, as will their daughters, but half the daughters will carry the gene for red–green color blindness. Half their daughters (grandchildren of the original color-blind man) will also be carriers; half their sons will be red–green color blind.

conception and birth rates, male versus female   Throughout the world, in every country and geographic area, more males than females are conceived. Some experts say that two boys are conceived for every girl; others say the ratio of boys to girls is only 120:100.

The birth statistics, however, are clear. Overall in the United States, there are 105 males born for every 100 females. The male/female ratio is similar in Great Britain, higher in Greece and Korea (113 males per 100 females), lower in Cuba (101 males per 100 females) and for African Americans (102.6 males for every 100 females). In the United States, the numbers seem to shift with the seasons—the disparity is higher in the spring, lower in the fall. In May, the month with the second highest birthrate, there are 106.2 newborn males for every 100 newborn females; in November, when the fewest babies are born, there are an average 104 boys for every 100 girls.

What makes this so interesting is that seminal fluid contains more X-bearing than Y-bearing sperm. Staining sperm cells with a fluorescent dye absorbed more readily by Y-bearing sperm, which then glow brighter than sperm carrying an X chromosome, Barry Bean, associate professor of biology at Lehigh University in Bethlehem, Pennsylvania, confirmed that the average ejaculation carries about ten X-bearing sperm for every nine Y-bearers. Nevertheless, year after year, studies show that there are only nine girls born for every ten boys, a net difference of about 0.2, which Bean calls a statistically hefty discrepancy.

Studies show similar ratios among embryos created *in vitro* for artificial insemination by adding sperm to a dish with a female egg. There are more X chromosomes in the seminal fluid, but the Y-bearing sperm seem to be more successful at reaching and penetrating the egg. The explanation seems to be that although Y-bearing sperm are more vulnerable to damage in the acidic environment of the vagina, they flourish in the alkaline cervix, uterus, and fallopian tubes. Thus if they make it past the vaginal canal, they are more likely to come out winners.

corpus callosum The corpus callosum is a group of fibers connecting the left and right hemispheres of the brain. In 1989, based on autopsies of 15 male and 35 female brains, Sandra Witelson of McMaster University in Hamilton, Ontario discovered that the isthmus, a narrow, bridgelike section at the rear of the corpus callosum, is larger in females than in males. In 1991, a team of University of California–Los Angeles scientists led by Roger Gorski and Laura Allen dissected 146 brains at autopsy and found the isthmus up to 23 percent bigger in women.

Based on autopsy examinations of 14 brains, Witelson has also found a second part of the corpus callosum, the splenum, to be larger in women. And UCLA researchers using magnetic resonance imaging (MRI) to measure brain anatomy in 29 living women say that the larger the splenum, the better the women performed on verbal fluency tests.

Because the corpus callosum connects the verbal and spatial thinking centers of the left and right hemispheres, it may be that women are better able than men to share functions between brain hemispheres. This ability to shift functions from one hemisphere to the other might explain not only the female advantage in LANGUAGE AND SPEECH, but also why girls are less susceptible to reading disabilities such as DYSLEXIA; why fewer left-handed women than men end up STUTTERING; and why women generally tend to recover faster and more fully from a STROKE involving the left side of the brain, where speech and verbal skills are centered.

D

death, ten leading causes   Every year in the United States, more men than women in every age group up to the very elderly, age 85+, succumb to the major illnesses and catastrophes that comprise the ten leading causes of death. The reasons given to explain this are generally the same ones used to explain why women as a group live longer than men: differences in the protective effects of the male and female SEX HORMONES, a stronger female IMMUNE SYSTEM, and cultural influences that discourage women from engaging in the risky or aggressive behavior that may lead to ACCIDENTS, SUICIDE, and HOMICIDE. [Note: For statistics on male versus female death rates from specific illnesses and conditions such as heart disease, see entries for each disease.]

TEN LEADING CAUSES OF DEATH
(MEN AND WOMEN), 1992

1. Diseases of the heart
2. Cancer
3. Cerebrovascular disease (stroke)
4. Chronic obstructive pulmonary diseases
5. Accidents
6. Pneumonia and influenza
7. Diabetes
8. HIV infections
9. Suicide
10. Homicide

Source: U.S. Centers for Disease Control, "Provisional numbers of deaths for the 10 leading causes of death by age, race and sex, United States, 1992," *Monthly Vital Statistics*, September 28, 1993.

TEN LEADING CAUSES OF REPORTED DEATHS
MEN VERSUS WOMEN, 1991

Men	Women
1. Heart diseases	1. Heart diseases
2. Cancer	2. Cancer
3. Accidents	3. Cerebrovascular disease
4. Cerebrovascular disease	4. Pneumonia/influenza
5. Chronic obstructive lung disease	5. Chronic obstructive lung disease
6. Pneumonia/influenza	6. Accidents
7. HIV infections	7. Diabetes
8. Suicide	8. Septicemia
9. Diabetes	9. Kidney disease
10. Homicide	10. Atherosclerosis

Source: National Center for Health Statistics, *Vital Statistics of the United States, 1991* (Washington, D.C., 1994).

---

death, time of   Examining the dates of death for 2,745,149 Californians who died of natural causes between 1969 and 1990, University of California–San Diego sociologist David P. Phillips discovered that, depending on a person's gender, birthdays, like other holidays, tend to serve as either symbolic "lifelines" or "deadlines."

Overall, people are more likely to die during the six days surrounding their birthdays than at any other time during the year, but men are more likely to die right before the birthday, women, right after. Women seem to be able somehow to prolong their lives briefly until they have reached what Phillips calls a "positive, meaningful occasion." In contrast, the peaks in male death rates shortly before the birthday suggest that men are more likely to think of their birthdays as negative markers. "Birthdays are an occasion to evaluate past achievements and future prospects," says Phillips. "Depending on your perspective and gender, it seems, you are likely to either look forward to or dread this anniversary."

In previous studies, Phillips also found cultural differences in death rates at anniversaries. Deaths among Jews, for example, seem to dip nearly a third below normal in the week before Passover and to rise by the same amount in the week after the holiday ends. A parallel study of Chinese mortality in the days before and after specific Chinese holidays showed exactly the same pattern.

depression   In the United States, the lifetime risk of major depression is 12 percent for a man and 15 percent for a woman. Overall, women are more likely than men to suffer from a mild depression, particularly in the middle years, between 35 and 45. After that, as they grow older, women's risk declines, and men's rises.

To date, attempts to explain this well-known difference in risk between the sexes have focused on cultural or hormonal factors—that is, on the way women think and the way their bodies behave. According to Robert M. Sapolsky, a MacArthur Fellow and the author of *Why Zebras Don't Get Ulcers*, a guide to how stress affects the body, blaming depression on thought processes ignores the fact that women are particularly prone to depression at times in their lives when their hormonal status is in flux: during menstruation, at menopause, during pregnancy and birth, or when they are using a product such as a birth control pill that artificially alters hormone levels.

Female hormones, particularly estrogen, affect brain chemistry, including the metabolism of neurotransmitters such as serotonin that impact on EMOTION and mood. In addition, studies show that women are more sensitive than men to antidepressant drugs and require smaller amounts to relieve depression, hinting at gender differences in how the brain produces and/or uses naturally occurring neurochemicals as well.

Finally, there is the fact that a woman's brain may simply be wired differently than a man's when it comes to reacting to thoughts or actions that provoke feelings of sadness that escalate to depression. Positron emission tomography (PET) is a form of radiography that produces an image based on particles called photons absorbed from radioactive material injected into the body. Using PET scans, psychiatrist Mark George of the National Institute of Mental Health measured brain activity for ten women and ten men who were asked to think sad thoughts—to think, for example, about a woman hearing her husband ask her for a divorce or a small boy standing at his father's funeral. Both men and women showed brain activity in the front of the limbic system, a part of the brain that has some control over the endocrine glands and over automatic responses such as breathing and heartbeat, as well as emotion. But in women, the area that was active when thinking sad thoughts was eight times larger than in men.

Paradoxically, when a person is seriously depressed, this part of the brain seems to be unresponsive. Perhaps, George speculates, a brain (male or female) that reacts so strongly and so often to the ordinary sad moments of life somehow exhausts its ability to cope with depressing events and thus is more susceptible to depressive illness.

diabetes   Diabetes is the seventh leading cause of death in the United States, directly responsible for approximately 50,000 deaths a year. Adding in deaths

REPORTED DEATHS FROM DIABETES, 1991

Age	Male	Female
All ages (yrs.)	21,096	27,855
1–14	*	*
15–34	*	342
35–54	2,578	2,009
55–74	9,850	10,995
75+	8,209	14,485

*Diabetes does not rank among the top ten causes of death in this age group.

Source: National Center for Health Statistics, *Vital Statistics of the United States, 1991* (Washington, D.C.: Public Health Service, 1994).

from complications such as kidney and cardiovascular disease, which are often considered separately, might raise that number to more than 300,000.

Diabetes is more common among women than among men, among people with more body fat, and among pregnant women, particularly those who are overweight. Because women are more likely to have diabetes, they are also more likely to suffer from its side effects, including retinal damage leading to blindness.

direction, finding   Ask a woman how to get to Bloomingdale's, and she's likely to tell you to walk two blocks past that big building on the corner, while a man will tell you to head north, up four blocks.

ESTIMATED DEATHS FROM DIABETES, 1992

Age	Male	Female
1–14 yrs.	—	40
15–24	50	20
25–34	350	240
35–44	920	630
45–54	1,890	1,420
55–64	3,770	3,670
65–74	6,510	7,630
75–84	6,090	9,170
85+	2,460	5,330

Source: U.S. Centers for Disease Control, "Provisional numbers of deaths for the 10 leading causes of death by age, race and sex, United States, 1992," *Monthly Vital Statistics*, September 28, 1993.

In other words, when it comes to finding their way, on foot or in a car, by ship and plane, women remember landmarks, while men appear to operate on an innate sense of compass readings and an estimate of how far they have come. (They're also better at reading maps.)

In one study at the University of Rochester in upstate New York, male and female students were blindfolded, walked through a series of underground tunnels, then asked to point the direction to a specific site, such as a building on the college campus. The women appeared to have been confused by the twists and turns of the walk through the maze, but the men were sufficiently well-oriented to give specific direction such as, "Through that door, to the left, turn right," and so on.

This superior ability to orient oneself in space may well arise from the more acute male sense of SPATIAL REASONING. In other words, the same inborn skill that makes men better at visualizing the various aspects of an object rotating in space may also allow them to "see" the way from here to there on an imaginary map, while a woman relies on details such as a specific building.

diverticulosis   Diverticulosis is a condition characterized by the formation of small pouches in weakened sections of the intestines. An infection in one of these pouches is called diverticulitis. Left untreated, the infection may spread to create an abscess in the wall of the bowel, perforate the bowel, or cause peritonitis, a general infection of the lining of the abdominal cavity. Diverticulitis may be treated with antibiotics or surgery to remove the inflamed, infected pouch. In one recent study of patients treated surgically, among people younger than 50 who require surgical treatment, men outnumber women three to one. After age 70, the ratio is exactly reversed, with three women patients for every man.

doctors, attitudes (male versus female)   In 1992, Edith B. Gross, professor of psychology at Beaver College in Pennsylvania, interviewed 72 physicians to find out what they considered the most stressful part of being a doctor. She discovered more similarities than differences between the men and the women.

Both male and female doctors are workaholics. Both worry about the time demands of a job that can take 60 hours a week or more. Both enjoy exercising authority, and both welcome the responsibility that comes with making life-and-death decisions. As a result, there is no indication that men who become doctors perform better than women who become doctors, or vice versa. But the increase in the number of women attending medical school and moving into the medical professions has given rise to studies describing differences in the way male and female doctors relate to their patients, specifically in the length of time they spend with them and the kind of conversation they encourage.

Analyzing tapes from visits between doctors and patients, Rita Charon, assistant professor of clinical medicine at Columbia University's College of Physicians and Surgeons, found that women doctors are more attentive. "They ask more questions, they give more information, and they demonstrate more support and there is more shared decision making."

"Women doctors use more positive terms, compliments, agreements and partnership statements," says Debra Roter, professor of health policy and management of the School of Hygiene and Public Health at Johns Hopkins University. "They talk more to their patients who talk more back to them." In a study similar to Charon's, Roter and her coauthors found that, on average, female doctors spend at least five minutes more in conversation with their patients than male doctors do. These longer interviews are not idle talk. They give the doctor valuable information about the patient's health, and they give the patient a feeling of participation. Overall, the longest doctor–patient interviews in Roter's study were between women doctors and women patients; the shortest, between male doctors and female patients. So women who complain that male doctors do not listen to them seem to have a case.

Women patients may also be short-changed by male doctors when it comes to the quality of medical care. Documenting the differences in cancer-screening practices between male and female primary care doctors treating more than 94,000 women patients at a large Minneapolis health organization, researchers found that women internists and women family practitioners were consistently more likely than their male cohorts to do Pap smears and breast examinations and to recommend mammograms. But the study showed virtually no difference in treatment practices between male and female gynecologists—the doctors most women consider their primary care physicians.

doctors, ratio of male versus female   In 1970, only 11 percent of all the doctors in the United States were women; by 1990, it was 22 percent. In 1994, for the first time ever, there were more female than male obstetrician/gynecologists coming into the medical profession. According to the American College of Obstetricians and Gynecologists (ACOG), the organization to which more than nine of every ten American obstetrician/gynecologists belong, almost 60 percent of the 1,312 new doctors beginning their four-year residencies in obstetrics/gynecology are women. By 1995, more female than male college freshmen planned to go to medical school.

Down's syndrome   The most common inherited form of mental retardation, Down's syndrome is a BIRTH DEFECT caused by a single extra chromosome. While there is no clear difference in the numbers of boys versus girls born with Down's syndrome, the defect is more common among children born to older mothers. The age of the father appears to be irrelevant.

DuPuytren's contracture   DuPuytren's contracture, named for the French physician who first described it in 1834, is a painless thickening and tightening of bands of fibrous tissue just under the skin on the palms of the hands. As the tissue contracts, the fingers are deformed, sometimes to the point where they can no longer flex and function.

DuPuytren's contracture sometimes follows repeated minor injuries to the hand. It is more common after age 40, and among alcoholics, people with epilepsy, pulmonary tuberculosis, diabetes, and liver disease. For unknown reasons, it is also more common among men.

dyslexia   Dyslexia is a READING disorder, a neurological dysfunction that makes it difficult for people of average or better-than-average intelligence to recognize symbols (letters and numerals) and translate them into words and numbers.

Dyslexia is commonly believed to affect boys more frequently than girls. Some experts dispute this, but there are at least two intriguing avenues of research to explain why this should be so.

The first is a recently discovered gender difference in brain anatomy. The CORPUS CALLOSUM is a bundle of nerve cells connecting the left and right hemispheres of the brain. Recent studies show that the female corpus callosum is larger than the male. It is entirely possible that their larger corpus callosum allows girls to shift functions more easily between the hemispheres, compensating for any defect that would trip a boy into dyslexia.

There also seems to be a genetic component to dyslexia. In 1994, a team of statistical geneticists at Sequana Therapeutics in La Jolla, California released a report of a study involving two groups of children, the first consisting of 114 pairs of sisters and/or brothers from families with a history of dyslexia, the other consisting of 50 pairs of fraternal twins, at least one of whom had a record of reading disorders. Genetic analysis showed that the children with learning disabilities all shared a distinctive DNA pattern on chromosome six. Now the search is on to identify the gene(s) that may be linked to reading disorders.

E

ears Because a man's head is usually bigger than a woman's, his ears are also likely to be noticeably larger.

They're hairier, too. Hair on the outer rims of the ears is an exclusively male trait, one of the very few inherited characteristics currently known to be carried on the Y chromosome.

eating disorders Eating disorders are virtually unknown in areas of the world where food is scarce. However, in the United States and Western Europe, where food is abundant, eating disorders affect a small but significant minority of the population, primarily adolescent girls. Among the general population, eating disorders are as much as ten times as common among women as among men, but boys who become anorexic exhibit the same obsession with body size that characterizes female anorexia. The single exception to the rule may be among athletes, especially runners and dancers, who—regardless of gender—seek constantly to reduce body fat.

The two most common eating disorders are ANOREXIA NERVOSA and BU-LIMIA. The first is a refusal to eat due to an irrational, overwhelming fear of obesity; the second, an attempt to control weight by voluntarily vomiting or using laxatives after meals. Although they seem contradictory, the two disorders often occur together in the same person.

emotion How human beings react emotionally may depend on a wide variety of psychological and cultural influences that create informal but widely accepted rules about how people should behave in emotionally charged situations. In Western culture, women have traditionally been described as warmer, more emotional, and less controlled than men.

At the same time, as the understanding of human physiology has expanded, scientists have come to understand that physiological factors, such as the presence or absence of sex hormones, can affect behavior, but this is usually interpreted in a way that conforms with the cultural norms. For example, estrogen, rather than the aggression-promoting testosterone, is regarded as the "emotional" hormone.

The growing use of imaging techniques such as magnetic resonance imaging (MRI) and positron emission tomography (PET) has allowed researchers to observe activity in the human brain. This has shown that men and women use their brains differently for LANGUAGE AND SPEECH and for READING.

Now there is imaging evidence to show that male and female brains may also behave differently in response to emotional cues. In 1995, using MRI to observe metabolic activity in the brains of 37 men and 24 women at rest, a team of researchers led by Ruben C. Gur, director of the University of Pennsylvania School of Medicine brain behavior laboratory, found a measurable difference in activity in the male and female limbic system, a group of structures in the brain that exert some effect over endocrine glands and the autonomic system that controls involuntary processes such as breathing and heartbeat.

The MRI images of male brains showed more activity in the parts of the limbic system involved with direct action, while women have more activity in the parts involved in symbolic action. The distinction, says Gur, is that "if a dog is angry and jumps and bites, that's an action. If he is angry and bares his fangs and growls, that's more symbolic."

In an earlier study, Gur found evidence to suggest that the sexes may interpret emotional stimuli differently. While men and women were equally able to recognize happiness in pictures of others, men were less able than women to recognize sadness in a woman's facial expression. Women, on the other hand, were good at identifying sadness in the faces of men as well as women.

exercise   The American Heart Association and the National Center for Health Statistics (NCHS) agree that in the United States men are more likely than women to exercise on a regular basis. Heart Association research shows 44 percent of American men exercising on a regular basis. NCHS numbers for men are slightly lower: 40 percent claim to engage in sports or vigorous exercise for 15 minutes three or more times a week. The number is higher (62 percent) among young men age 18 to 24 and lower (38 percent) for men age 45 to 64 or older than 65 (32 percent).

Women are less active. American Heart Association statistics show that only 38 percent of American women engage in regular exercise. This number is roughly confirmed by a 1995 report from the Centers for Disease Control in Atlanta showing that nearly three-quarters of American women do not get enough exercise; statistically the least active are black women.

For men, strenuous exercise is almost always beneficial. For women, its benefits may be dose-related. Exercise develops muscle and depletes body fat. A healthy woman's body requires a minimum amount of body fat in order to sustain reproductive function. Highly trained women athletes—most commonly runners and dancers—who exercise strenuously may reduce body fat to a level that will not meet this requirement. The result? They stop menstruating.

However, there is a whole body of evidence to suggest that regular, moderate weight-bearing exercises such as walking, running, jogging, lifting weights, and stair climbing, in conjunction with appropriate calcium and vitamin D intakes, protects bone mass in postmenopausal women and may reduce the incidence or severity of osteoporosis in older women.

eyebrows and eyelashes   Eyebrows and eyelashes are clear exceptions to the rule that a person's sex hormones decide the placement and patterns of body and facial hair. Poets and lovers notwithstanding, long, lush lashes are not an exclusively female characteristic, nor are bushy eyebrows solely a male feature. Eyelashes may be thick or sparse regardless of gender, and with advancing age, the hair in both male and female eyebrows is likely to grow longer and more unruly.

There is certainly a genetic component at work here. Blood relatives usually have similar facial features, including the amount and pattern of the hair around and above the eyes. Parents with long lashes and bushy eyebrows, or short lashes and sparse eyebrows, or any combinations thereof, will pass the same patterns on to their offspring.

eyelids, swollen   Absent injury or disease, a puffy swelling of the eyelids is most often the result of temporary fluid retention caused by an allergic reaction or, in women, fluctuating hormone levels during the menstrual cycle. Either way, swollen eyelids are likely to recur over a period of years, more frequently in women than in men.

F

Fabry's disease   Fabry's disease is a rare, inherited, X-LINKED disorder of fat metabolism characterized by corneal opacity (cataract), fevers, pain in the arms and legs and potentially fatal high blood pressure. As with other X-linked traits, full-blown Fabry's disease occurs primarily in men. Women who have one X chromosome with the gene for Fabry's disease are protected by their second, healthy X chromosome. Their most common symptom is cataract.

fat   The fetus develops fat tissue late in pregnancy, during the last trimester. Therefore, infants born premature may not have time to accumulate sufficient body fat to maintain body heat; they must be protected in warmed incubators. More boys than girls are born premature, so, like their full-term brothers, more premature boys are born without sufficient body fat.

Even full-term boys are born with less fat tissue than girls. Studies measuring newborns with calipers that pinch the skin at the upper arm midway between shoulder and elbow or on the back, just below the shoulder blade, show this difference to be consistent regardless of race, ethnicity, or length of pregnancy.

In the first few months of life, male–female differences in fat and muscle tissue remain small but noticeable. They grow more pronounced through childhood. By the time they get to puberty, girls—with their budding breasts and widening hips—clearly have more fat than boys. In young adulthood, the female body is 20–25 percent fat; the male body, 15–20 percent fat. In old age, both men and women lose muscle and gain fat.

A woman's fat, stored at breast, hip, and thigh, is not mere decoration. Although new (1995) data from the long-running Nurses Health Study at Boston suggest that women who gain significant amounts of weight as they grow older may be at increased risk of HEART DISEASE, women who maintain reasonable

50

amounts of padding are less likely than their skinny sisters to end up with OSTEOPOROSIS. The fat pads provide material protection for bones, while serving as a site for the synthesis of estrogen no longer secreted by the ovaries.

In the United States, where thinness is the ideal, even normal female fat may trigger psychological problems ranging from EATING DISORDERS such as ANO-REXIA NERVOSA and BULIMIA to a poor self-image. In a 1988 study of 98 men and 128 women in their freshman year at the University of Michigan, researchers Adam Drewnowski and Doris K. Yee found that 90 percent of the normal-weight women they interviewed wanted to lose weight, a finding that seems to be typical. Yet only half the normal-weight men wanted to weigh less; 30 percent wanted to weigh more, probably because large body size in males is associated with muscle, not fat.

feet   At birth, small as it is, a baby's foot has 35 joints, 19 muscles, more than 100 ligaments, and cartilage that will eventually become 26 separate and distinct bones. Feet continue to grow until they are fully developed, a point that is reached at about age 14–16 for girls, 15–21 for boys.

Then the feet stop growing, at least for a while. They stay about the same size and shape until early middle age. Around age 30 for a woman and 40 for a man, as years of bearing the body's weight stretch ligaments and cause bones to shift slightly, people often find themselves shopping for new, larger shoes in which to walk comfortably into old age.

fertility   Fertility is the ability to conceive children. Perhaps the most impor-tant difference between male and female reproductive function is the fact that men remain fertile for a much longer period of time.

A man is fertile as long as he continues to produce sufficient quantities of healthy sperm—at least 20 million to 100 million sperm in a milliliter of ejaculate. While sperm production does decline with age, in theory (and some-times in vigorous reality) a man may be fertile as long as he lives.

Women, on the other hand, are fertile for approximately 30 to 40 years, from puberty to menopause, at which time the ovaries no longer release an egg a month. New technologies, including the implanting of a fertilized egg into a woman's uterus, can make postmenopausal pregnancy (but not fertility) a reality. In December 1993, a 59-year-old British woman gave birth to twins after fertilized eggs had been implanted in her uterus at an Italian clinic; in July 1992, Rossana Della Corte, a 62-year-old Italian woman, became the world's oldest new mother after the same treatment was performed at the same Italian clinic. One month later, in response, the French parliament proposed a law to restrict artificial fertilization in older women. They argued that being pregnant late in life is hazardous to the woman and immoral in its consequences for her child.

fetus, sex of   Gender matters, even in the womb. As early as the fourth month of pregnancy, when high levels of testosterone and gonadotropins (hormones that promote the growth of ovaries and testes) are circulating through the male fetus, a pregnant woman carrying a male fetus will have gained more weight and will have higher BLOOD PRESSURE than a woman carrying a female fetus. She is also more likely to have suffered a MISCARRIAGE, perhaps because males are more susceptible than females to inherited birth defects.

The simplest explanation for the differences in maternal weight and blood pressure is the male fetus's supply of testosterone. Testosterone is an anabolic steroid hormone that promotes tissue growth; it also increases sodium and water retention. Women carrying male fetuses also have a greater flow of blood across the placenta into the uterus—not an unmixed blessing. A higher blood flow to the fetus reduces the risk of stillbirth, but it also retards the maturation of the fetal lungs and slows the production of a foamy fluid known as surfactant that enables lung tissue to expand and contract, protecting a premature infant from respiratory distress syndrome (RDS).

RDS is more common among premature boys than among premature girls. President John F. Kennedy's second son, Patrick Bouvier Kennedy, a premature baby, died of RDS within a few days of his birth in the summer of 1963, just months before his father's assassination. Since then, doctors have identified a component in amniotic fluid that warns of lung immaturity in an infant whose mother is about to go into premature labor. Giving the mother adrenal hormones may speed maturing of the baby's lungs. In addition, the introduction of

---

FACTORS ASSOCIATED WITH CARRYING A MALE FETUS

1. Shorter pregnancy
2. More weight gain
3. Higher blood flow to the fetus
4. No increase in proteinuria of pregnancy (protein in the urine of an otherwise healthy person)
5. Increased risk of maternal high blood pressure
6. Increased incidence of swelling of the hands and face
7. More likely to be carried by women who have had previous pregnancies

Source: Richard L. Naeye and Nebiat Tafari, *Risk Factors in Pregnancy and Diseases of the Fetus and Newborn* (Baltimore: Williams & Wilkins, 1983).

replacement surfactant in 1989 has made it possible to treat infants with RDS and thereby substantially improve their chances of survival.

finger length   Like the larger male SKULL, the pointed female chin, and the longer male ARM and LEG bones, finger length is a gender-related characteristic. Right from birth, a girl's second (index) finger tends to be longer than her fourth (ring) finger, while a boy's second finger is generally shorter than his fourth. There is no known explanation for this lifelong difference.

fingerprints   A fingerprint is made up of four principle types of patterns: the arch (which looks something like the layers of rock underneath a hill); the loop (which looks something like a U with the round, close end pointed towards the thumb); the whorl; and the composite (a group of loops and forks). It is probably impossible to identify gender from fingerprints, but in general, a woman's is likely to have more arches and fewer whorls.

food cravings   In the five years between 1989 and 1994, more than 50 scientific papers were published on the subject of food cravings—the insistent desire for specific foods. The studies confirm what most people knew by instinct: on average, women crave sweets, and men crave meat.

In a 1991 survey of food cravings among 1,000 undergraduates at McMaster University in Hamilton, Ontario, 97 percent of the women and 67 percent of the men admitted experiencing specific food cravings. While both craved fat, the women seemed to prefer to get their fat from sweets (i.e., CHOCOLATE), the men, from protein foods (i.e., steaks, hamburger, and seafood). A similar study at Monell Chemical Senses Center in Philadelphia produced similar results. Young women chose high-fat sweets (chocolate again) by a margin of two to one. Young men chose high-protein main dishes by precisely the same margin.

Some cravings appear to be nutritionally based. For example, pica—the repeated consumption of nonnutritive substances such as clay—may reflect a need for minerals such as iron. But there is a strong case to be made for a hormonal influence. For example, the male craving for protein foods may be activated by higher levels of the muscle-building male sex hormone testosterone. The female craving for carbohydrates, which activate brain chemicals that increase a sense of well-being, appears to rise and fall along with levels of female hormones during the phases of the menstrual cycle.

So do the well-known food cravings of pregnancy. Patricia Pline, professor of social psychology at the University of Toronto, suggests that pregnancy-related food cravings are protective and health-related, noting that the foods most frequently preferred are fruit, fruit juices, chocolate, and dairy products.

Do these hormonal connections mean that men and women are actually born craving different foods? Maybe. Some studies of newborns have shown a clear female preference for sweet liquids; others have shown no difference at all. Current research suggests that as men and women age, their cravings become more similar, but never quite equal.

fragile X syndrome   Fragile X syndrome is an inherited X-LINKED TRAIT named for a gap (fragile site) at the end of the long arm of the X chromosome. The syndrome, first identified in 1991, is the most common type of inherited mental retardation, second only to DOWN'S SYNDROME as a cause of mental retardation in boys. It occurs in one of every 2,000 male births. Ten to 15 percent of males with autism, a mysterious condition once considered a form of child-hood schizophrenia, carry the fragile X trait.

G

gallbladder disease The gallbladder is a small sac linked by ducts to the liver and the small intestine. It serves as a storage site for bile, a substance that enables the body to digest fats.*

There are two common forms of gallbladder disease: gallstones and inflammation of the gallbladder. Both are three to four times more common among women. There is an indisputable hormone connection: A woman's risk of gallstones and gallbladder disease rises when she is overweight, pregnant, or using birth control pills, and doubles while she is using postmenopausal hormone replacement therapy.

Eight of every ten Americans with gallstones have stones made of cholesterol; the other two have pigment stones, made of bile pigments such as bilirubin. The risk of cholesterol gallstones is higher when a person is on a crash diet, because the diet increases the body's production of cholesterol. Pigment stones occur more frequently among people with liver disease or a condition that continuously destroys red blood cells, releasing their pigments into the bloodstream. One example of this type of condition is sickle cell anemia, which occurs almost exclusively among African Americans. For unknown reasons, pigment stones are also more common among people of Asian descent.

germ cells The body contains two kinds of cells, somatic cells and germ cells. Somatic cells, which comprise all our organs and tissues, evolve in dizzying variety from the single cell of the fertilized egg. Germ cells evolve from the sac surrounding the yolk.

---

*Bile, which is manufactured in the liver, is 82 percent water, plus acids (cholic acid, which comprises 12 percent of bile, is one), fat-and-phosphorus compounds such as lecithin (4 percent of bile), and cholesterol (0.7 percent). It also contains the red pigment bilirubin, assorted proteins, potassium, sodium, and mucus.

Both somatic cells and germ cells reproduce by mitosis, first doubling their genes and chromosomes and then splitting into two new cells with exactly the same genetic material as the original. Through mitosis, germ cells produce spermatocytes and oocytes, which then go through a second kind of division, called meiosis.

Meiosis is a reduction division. It creates cells—sperm and eggs (also known as germ cells)—with half the normal number of chromosomes, so that when sperm meets egg they come together to make a cell with a normal complement of genes and chromosomes, half from the egg, half from the sperm.

By the end of the second month of pregnancy, a female fetus's ovaries begin to form estrogen. About one month later, the estrogen signals germ cells in the developing ovary to begin producing oocytes. By the seventh month, when mitotic division of the germ cells ends, there are about 7,000,000 oocytes in the fetal ovaries. Then oocytes begin to die off; when the baby is born, she will have only about 200,000 left, all "frozen" at the stage right before meiotic division. At puberty, rising estrogen secretion once again triggers the start of meiotic division, which this time leads to the release of one mature egg each month until menopause.

In a male fetus, germ cells in the fetal testes continue mitotic division right up until the moment of birth. Then mitosis stops. It will begin again at puberty when testosterone levels increase.

As a result, all the eggs a woman will ever have are present in her ovaries when she is born, but a healthy man continues to produce new sperm throughout his adult life. As a result, no egg comes from a cell that has been through more than 35 mitotic divisions. But by the time a man is fifty, the sperm he ejaculates (between 20 and 110 million per milliliter of seminal fluid) comes from germ cells that may have gone through more than 500 mitotic divisions. Each time a cell goes through mitosis, there is a chance that the DNA in its genes will mutate spontaneously or be damaged while the cell is dividing.

Even in the absence of outside influences such as chemicals or radiation, the odds are that sperm are more likely than eggs to end up with a mutation in a single gene. On the other hand, eggs are more likely to end up with too many chromosomes, or too few, as a result of the chromosomes' failure to separate properly during meiosis. So the kinds of BIRTH DEFECTS likely to be transmitted by mother and father differ. Women are more likely to pass on defects such as DOWN'S SYNDROME that are due to the presence of, absence of, or damage to an entire chromosome; men, defects such as MARFAN'S SYNDROME that are due to the presence of, absence of, or damage to a single gene.

gout   Gout is a form of ARTHRITIS in which the body either produces too much or excretes too little uric acid. As a result, sharp crystals of uric acid collect at joints in the extremities, most commonly the big toe. Less commonly, the crystals may aggregate and solidify into uric acid kidney stones. Either way, they can cause excruciating pain, and when the big toe aches from gout, the odds are nine to one it's a male toe.

Gout may run in families, and it seems to be hormone-related. As the Greek physician Hippocrates noted more than 2,500 years ago, it rarely occurs in eunuchs, sexually immature men, or premenopausal women. This observation, which parallels Aristotle's on BALDNESS, may testify to the protective effect of male hormones.

Graves' disease   Graves' disease is a relatively common form of hyperthyroidism, an abnormality of the thyroid gland leading to increased secretion of thyroid hormones. Its symptoms include goiter (a swollen thyroid gland); a quickened heartbeat and/or and palpitations; increased sweating; increased appetite with a paradoxical weight loss; insomnia; diarrhea; and swollen, teary, irritated, staring eyes with droopy eyelids.

Graves' disease is most commonly diagnosed in the 20s and 30s, but it may appear at any age—Barbara Bush, wife of President George Bush, was diagnosed in her 60s. The ratio of women to men patients is as high as seven or eight women to every man. There is some evidence that Graves' disease runs in families; what sets it off in any one individual is still unknown.

growth   Until they are about nine years old, boys and girls are generally equal in size and strength. Then a period of sudden growth called the "growth spurt" changes the picture.

For girls, the growth spurt commonly begins between age 9 and 12; for boys, it starts about two years later. At first girls pull sharply ahead. Their bones lengthen, they shoot up in height, they put on weight and muscle mass, and their organs (with the exception of the lymphatics, which decrease in size) grow larger. A girl grows taller fastest between age 11 and 12, when she is likely to be shooting up at the rate of three inches a year. Boys grow at peak velocity—sometimes up to four inches a year—between age 13 and 14. In the same time period, both girls and boys may double their weight.

Because girls begin to grow earlier than boys, the average 12-year-old girl is likely to be taller than the average 12-year-old boy and may outweigh him by as much as six pounds. The situation will, of course, reverse itself over the next few years when the boys reach PUBERTY, slightly later than the girls. Although the two-to-four-year growth spurt comes earlier for girls, it lasts longer for boys. By age 18, when growth is 99 percent complete for girls, boys have about an inch left to go. In adulthood, men generally end up heavier and taller than women.

H

hair   Where human beings grow hair depends on their gender. Male and female patterns of body hair are secondary sex characteristics dictated by the SEX HORMONES, estrogen and testosterone. Although some ethnic groups, such as Asians, are less hairy than others, men are hairier than women regardless of race or ethnicity.

When female hormones dominate, the face and chest remain relatively smooth except for several hairs around the nipples, and the pubic hair grows in the shape of an inverted triangle. When male hormones dominate, the face is whiskery, the chest and shoulders may be furry, and the pubic patch is shaped like a diamond. With age, as women produce less estrogen and men less testosterone, the balance shifts.

An elderly man's BEARD may thin out, while an elderly woman may sprout hair on her chin and upper lip; both lose hair under the arms and in the pubic area. How much hair they gain or lose as the hormones shift depends to some extent on their genes; similar patterns do run in families.

Because hair growth is linked to sex hormones, it is interesting to note that, with the possible exception of the top of the head, the places nature has decorated with hair are the parts of the body that draw sexual attention, serving our most basic drive: the need to reproduce.

The hairy parts of the body are among those most sensitive to touch. At the base of every hair there are myriad nerve endings (touch receptors) to detect even the slightest movement. These receptors are so efficient that most mammalian animals, including cats and dogs, have long, sensitive whiskers around the nose that allow the animal to maneuver around obstacles even in a darkened room. In addition, the skin at hairy sites is generally thinner than at other places on the body and more sensitive to touch. That is why having the scalp massaged

59

can be a sensuous experience. For bald men, too—the receptors remain even after the hair is gone.

hair, graying   Silver threads among the gold: who'll find them first, a man or a woman?

According to a study by enterprising Australian researchers from the Anti-Cancer Council of Victoria and the Australian Red Cross, it's a draw. Neither gender affects how fast the hair turns gray, nor does it matter what the original hair color was.

At age 25, 22 percent to 29 percent of all men, and 23 percent to 34 percent of all women, have some gray hair, a difference so small it is considered insignificant. By age 45, there is a very slight male edge on being completely gray, but not enough to hang your hat on. As for hair color, the only difference in graying between blondes and brunettes is that early graying is more visible in dark hair because of the contrast, while later graying looks more complete in blondes because the gray hair blends in with the blonde to make it look gray overall.

Graying hair is not a health problem; people whose hair turns gray early in life are not at any greater risk for any medical problem. As a result, there has been very little serious follow-up to the 35-year-old Australian study. For example, no one has yet studied the effects of race, so there is no evidence as to whether it affects the rate at which the hair turns gray. But there is evidence to show that the tendency to graying is inherited. If your parents turned gray early, you are likely to, as well.

hands, cold   "Cold hands, warm heart" may not sound scientific, but it is an accurate description of the way women's bodies behave, particularly during the reproductive years.

Under normal circumstances, the TEMPERATURE in the body's inner core, where the organs rest, is slightly higher than the temperature of the skin. If the body is chilled, and the core temperature begins to fall, tiny blood vessels just under the skin constrict so that less warm blood flows up to the body's surface. As a consequence, there is less chilled blood flowing back to cool the center of the body. In extreme conditions, the spasms of the small blood vessels may lead to frostbite. In effect, the body sacrifices its extremities to protect its vital core.

This reaction is particularly acute in women, whose BLOOD VESSELS contract and expand more easily than a man's and who are more likely to have RAY-NAUD'S DISEASE, a condition that causes an intense reaction to cold.

handwriting   In one test of his skill, handwriting expert Albert S. Osborn of Osborn Document Examiners in New York told the *New York Times* that after looking through 5,000 sample cards he was able to identify the gender of the writer correctly 80 percent of the time. But that was "usually on the assumption that women write more neatly than men, and what good," he asked, "is 80 percent?"

Hansen's disease (leprosy)   Hansen's disease is a chronic infection of the skin and peripheral nerve tissue caused by a bacillus (*Mycobacterium leprae*). It is more common in warm countries, among poor people. In children, it occurs equally among boys and girls. Among adults, for unexplained reasons, the ratio of male to female patients is two to one.

Hashimoto's disease   Hashimoto's disease, also known as Hashimoto's thyroiditis, is a chronic thyroid inflammation that some believe is a disorder of the IMMUNE SYSTEM similar to arthritis in that the body appears to attack its own tissues. While GRAVES' DISEASE is the most common cause of hyperthyroidism (oversecretion of thyroid hormone), Hashimoto's is the most common cause of hypothyroidism (reduced secretion of thyroid hormone). It requires lifelong hormone replacement. Hashimoto's disease is most frequently diagnosed between age 30 and age 50, more commonly found in women than in men. As with Graves' disease, there may be a family history.

hay fever   It's ragweed season and somebody's sneezing. Is that somebody more likely to be a man or a woman? According to the National Center for Health Statistics, it's more likely to be a man, probably one aged 18 to 24.

Although people of every age may experience allergic symptoms, the percentage is highest among young adult males, 33 percent of whom wheeze and sneeze when they're exposed to animal hair, house dust, or pollen in the air. Only 18 percent of the women in this age group react the same way. However, women are more likely than men to be allergic to cats and dogs. No one knows why.

headache   Headache is the most common form of pain. In any given week, about 15 percent of all Americans have a headache, women more often than men.

Women are more likely to suffer from classic MIGRAINES; men, from the migraines known as cluster headaches. Tension headaches, triggered by spasms in the muscles at the shoulders and at the base of the skull, are an equal opportunity pain in the neck, as are sinus headaches and headaches resulting

---

PERCENT OF AMERICANS WHO SUFFER FROM HEADACHE OF ANY KIND

Age	Male	Female
18–24 yrs.	70%	84%
25–34	68	89
35–44	71	85
45–54	60	81
55–64	52	67
65–74	37	62
75–79	26	50

Source: National Center for Health Statistics.

---

from poor vision (squinting to see without the right glasses can set off painful spasms in the muscles of the eye).

For both men and women, headaches become less common with advancing age.

hearing   Every night at 2 A.M. when the new baby begins to cry, Dad sleeps straight through the wails. Is he just pretending to be asleep so he doesn't have to get up? Maybe not.

In studies conducted at the National Institutes of Health (NIH), researchers compared daily variations in sensory perception in men and women. They found that a woman's senses (hearing, taste, touch, vision, and smell) are generally sharper than a man's and respond more clearly to hormonal influences. An NIH study measuring the acuity of a woman's senses during a monthly cycle found them most acute at ovulation, when the estrogen level is at its highest.

There are also daily (circadian) variations. On average, says Robert Henkin, director of the Taste and Smell Clinic at the Center for Molecular Nutrition and Sensory Disorders in Washington, D.C., a woman's sense of hearing is sharpest during the early morning hours between 2 A.M. and 3 A.M. It is possible that nature built a hearing advantage into women's bodies specifically to make it easier for them to hear that hungry baby's cry. In fact, throughout the animal kingdom the simple sound of an infant's crying—a lamb's bleat, a puppy's yip, or a human baby's wail—triggers the secretion of prolactin, the hormone that stimulates milk production and a flow of milk into its sleeping mother's breast.

hearing loss   The scientific name for age-related hearing loss is presbycusis. The first symptom, which may appear as early as age 20, is a slight inability to hear sounds at the highest frequencies. This is followed by a gradual slide in acuity right down the frequency scale. By age 55 to 65, there is considerable variation in how well people hear. Some are considerably hard of hearing by age 50; others have no perceptible problems well into their 90s.

As a rule, men seem to be affected more often and more severely than women, but this is one of those cases where the statistics may be skewed by the culture. Does the higher incidence of hearing loss among men reflect a true sensory loss or does it reflect the fact that more men than women visit the doctor for hearing problems?

heart   Judging by heartbeat, a newborn boy's heart may be presumed to be larger than a newborn girl's. The difference would almost certainly arise from the fact that boys usually weigh more than girls at birth.

Unfortunately, the larger male heart is more likely to be damaged. The American Heart Association reports that the death rate from congenital heart defects is 2.5 for every 100,000 white males, 3.1 for every 100,000 black males, 2.1 for every 100,000 white females, and 2.6 for every 100,000 black females.

heartbeat   In the womb, the fetal heart beats a steady 130 to 160 times a minute. At birth, a newborn's heart beats 140 times a minute. It slows to 130 at one month; to 115 at one year; to 110 at two years; to 85 at 12 years; and to 82 at 18 years.

At every point, however, the female heart consistently beats about five more times per minute, and this pattern continues straight on into adulthood, when the normal resting adult pulse rate is 70–78 beats a minute for men, 75–85 for women.

The difference may be attributable to size. The average male heart weighs 10 ounces; the average female heart, 8 ounces. A smaller heart must beat faster (that is, more frequently to move along as much blood as a larger heart. At each beat, the heart takes in and sends out about ¼ pint of blood. At 74 beats a minute, an average male heart pumps 833 gallons of blood a day; at 80 beats a minute, the average female heart pumps 900 gallons a day.

heart bypass surgery   Coronary artery bypass surgery is more effective at relieving symptoms in men than in women. Women are more likely to have a higher recurrence of angina pain, perhaps because a woman's arteries, like her heart and indeed her entire body, are generally smaller than a man's.

heart disease   Heart disease is the leading killer in the United States, the reported cause of more deaths than any other disease, condition, or action.

Women have a lifelong advantage against heart disease. Even when their CHOLESTEROL levels are higher, their risk of heart attack is lower. There are fewer female deaths from heart disease every year in every age group up to age 75, when there are more women left alive and thus more female deaths.

Many have attributed this advantage to the protective effects of estrogen, pointing to the fact that the postmenopausal increase in the incidence of heart attacks among women correlates with falling estrogen production. But in the late 1960s and early 1970s, when the National Institutes of Health sponsored a project designed to see whether giving men estrogen would reduce their risk of heart disease, the experiment backfired dismally. Male volunteers who got low doses of estrogen (1.25 mg per day) showed no effects at all. Those who got high doses (2.5 mg per day) began to develop blood clots in their legs and lungs. In the end, the female protective factor (and how it might be useful for men) remained a mystery locked up as tight as Mona Lisa's smile.

In fact, recent studies suggest that the male hormone testosterone may be as protective for men as estrogen appears to be for women. In the fall of 1994, a team of researchers at St. Luke's–Roosevelt Hospital Center in New York City, led by Gerald B. Phillips, found that men with lower testosterone levels were at higher risk of coronary artery disease. Examining X-ray pictures of the arteries of 55 men, none of whom had yet had a heart attack, they found a significant

REPORTED DEATHS FROM HEART DISEASE, 1991*		
Age	**Male**	**Female**
All ages	359,814	361,048
1–14 yrs.	329	284
15–34	2,924	1,491
35–54	31,745	11,026
55–74	149,521	84,865
75+	174,625	263,041

Source: National Center for Health Statistics, *Vital Statistics of the United States, 1991* (Washington, D.C.: Public Health Service, 1994).

*The figures in this chart come from the National Center for Health Statistics. They include deaths from rheumatic fever/rheumatic heart disease, hypertensive heart disease, hypertensive heart and renal disease, pregnancy coronary artery disease, and diseases of pulmonary circulation. They exclude deaths from hypertension without kidney disease, stroke, atherosclerosis (hardening of the arteries), and other diseases of arteries, capillaries, veins, and lymphatics. Thus, the NCHS figures equal only three-fourths of all the deaths that the American Heart Association blames on cardiovascular causes. The AHA totals comprise deaths from coronary artery disease, hypertensive disease, rheumatic fever/rheumatic heart disease, and all cerebrovascular diseases.

ESTIMATED DEATHS FROM HEART DISEASE, 1992		
Age	Male	Female
Less than 1 yr.	300	290
1–14	300	250
15–24	620	350
25–34	2,110	1,010
35–44	9,450	3,240
45–54	23,400	7,500
55–64	49,650	22,530
65–74	95,990	61,330
75–84	111,710	118,110
85+	65,450	146,750

Source: U.S. Centers for Disease Control, "Provisional numbers of deaths for the 10 leading causes of death by age, race and sex, United States, 1992," *Monthly Vital Statistics*, September 28, 1993.

correlation between low hormone levels and blocked arteries. The correlation was strongest with levels of hormone not bound to protein—a form of testosterone considered biologically active, accounting for about 2 percent of all the testosterone in the body. There was also a positive correlation between testosterone and high-density LIPOPROTEINS (HDLs), the so-called "good" cholesterol, particles that carry cholesterol out of the body rather than into arteries, suggesting that testosterone influences the ratio of HDLs. The higher the levels of testosterone, the higher the levels of HDLs.

"Because heart disease was considered to be a man's disease," the researchers said, "it was generally assumed that testosterone is the provocative factor. Now just the opposite is true—testosterone may prevent coronary heart disease in men."

BODY SHAPE counts, too. The classic female "pear-shaped" body, larger around the hips than at the waist, appears to confer some protection against heart disease.

heart transplants   In the United States, most heart transplant patients are male. The average age of male transplant patients is 48; the average age of women who receive new hearts is 42.

Men are also likelier than women to be given the slightly more effective dual-chamber heart pacemaker, perhaps because of a gender bias on the part of the surgeon or because it is more difficult to implant the device in a smaller female body. Whose heart is transplanted may have some effect on how well the transplant succeeds (see ORGAN TRANSPLANTS).

height   At birth, boys are generally ⅓ to ⅖ of an inch longer than girls, and except for a few years in adolescence, when girls mature earlier and grow faster, the average male is taller than the average female.

In America, males reach a maximum median height of 5'10" sometime between ages 15 and 24; females reach a maximum median height of 5'5" sometime between ages 19 and 24. After that, height declines. By age 51, the maximum median height for men is 5'8"; for women, 5'3". In old age, bone loss and loss of muscle tone reduce height even further.

The tallest man whose height was reliably recorded was Robert Pershing Wadlow (1918–1940), of Alton, Illinois. On his 13th birthday, Wadlow stood 7'1¾"; at age 18, 8'1½". At his death, he was measured at 8'11¾".

The tallest woman in medical history was Zeng Jinlian (1964–1982), who measured 7'1½" at age 13. At the time of her death, she was assumed to be 8'1¾" tall, but that was a projection based on what her height would have been had she been able to stand up straight; in fact, she suffered from pronounced SCOLIOSIS (spinal curvature).

At the other end of the measuring tape, the world's shortest man appears to be Gul Mohammed, born in 1957 in Delhi, India. In 1990, Mr. Mohammed was measured at Ram Monohar Hospital in New Delhi, where he was reported to be 22½" tall. He weighed in at 37½ pounds. The shortest woman on record was a Dutch citizen named Pauline Musters (1876–1895). Ms. Musters measured 24" at her death, but since she was lying stretched out at the time, this is assumed to be a bit greater than her living height.

Height is influenced by many genes from both parents. Given the multiplicity of genes involved, it is virtually impossible to predict the height of any particular individual, but overall it is safe to bet that the average adult male will end up taller than the average adult female. The male height advantage is so deeply ingrained in our consciousness that since the introduction of growth hormones to treat excessively short children, parents bring boys for treatment nearly twice as often as girls.

Height may also be affected by environmental factors, including diet. Occasionally, very short stature is due to a genetic defect. Turner's syndrome, the absence of one X chromosome, produces short girls with a variety of physical problems, including heart and kidney abnormalities. Noonan's syndrome, a trait carried by a dominant gene, causes mental retardation and heart defects in both boys and girls; boys with Noonan's syndrome are also likely to have a smaller-than-normal penis and undescended testicles.

There is no denying the advantages of being tall. Not only can you see what's happening on stage from any seat in the house; you may also get to see it for a longer period of time. On average, tall people are less likely than short people to have heart attacks. According to a mid-1980s study by Patricia Hebert of Brigham and Women's Hospital in Boston, a man who is 5'7" or shorter has a risk of heart attack one-third higher than that of a man who is 6'1" or taller. Hebert's tentative conclusion is based on five years of follow-up for 22,071 male and female doctors enrolled in the Physicians Health Study there. A similar study at the Slone Epidemiology Unit of Boston University turned up similar results for women. One possible (but unproven) explanation: Short people have narrower blood vessels that are more likely to be clogged by a passing blood clot.

hemophilia   Hemophilia, a disorder in which blood lacks the factors required for clotting, is an X-LINKED TRAIT—a trait carried on the X chromosome. It occurs in about one in every 3,000 to 5,000 American males.

The sons of a man with hemophilia and a woman who does not carry the gene are not at risk because they inherit their father's Y chromosome, not his X. His daughters, however, get one X chromosome from him, so they are carriers. Every son born to these daughters has a 50 percent chance of getting the hemophilia gene and the disorder; every daughter has a 50 percent chance of inheriting the gene and becoming a carrier. To develop hemophilia herself, a female must inherit a defective X gene from both her mother and her father.

hiccups   A hiccup is what happens when an involuntary spasm of the diaphragm is accompanied by an involuntary closing of the glottis, the opening at the back of the mouth that leads to the throat. Shutting the glottis stops air from flowing in the throat and produces the characteristic hiccup sound, somewhere between a gulp and a click.

Hiccups may start after a trivial irritation such as that caused by swallowing hot or irritating food, or they may arise from a variety of medical conditions including (but definitely not limited to) pleurisy, pneumonia, chest surgery, kidney disease, alcoholism, abdominal surgery, bowel disease, pancreatitis, pregnancy, bladder irritation, hepatitis, liver cancer, and certain brain tumors.

In mild cases, home remedies usually suffice. Breathing into a paper bag, for example, increases the level of carbon dioxide in the blood, causing the brain to signal the diaphragm to contract more deeply so as to bring more air into the body and more oxygen into the blood. The deepened contractions of the diaphragm may end the spasms. So may the sharp intake of breath caused by drinking from "the wrong side of the glass," or having someone sneak up behind and go, "Boo."

The simplest medical treatments for hiccups are usually embellished versions of the home remedies: inhaling a mixture of carbon dioxide and oxygen rather than breathing into a paper bag, washing out the stomach instead of drinking from a glass of water. Occasionally, these do not suffice, and the hiccup spasms may continue for hours, days, weeks, months, or years, making it hard to eat, sleep or even breathe properly. If this happens, doctors may recommend surgery to cut the nerve so that the muscles cannot spasm.

Hiccups are more common among men than among women, so it is not surprising that the champion for long-running hiccups is a man, Charles Osborne, of Anthon, Iowa, who began hiccupping in 1922 and kept it up for 69 years and 5 months, a hiccup every 1.5 seconds until February 1990, when he suddenly stopped. From then until his death on May 1, 1991, there is no record of his ever having hiccupped again.

high blood pressure (hypertension)   Blood pressure is the force exerted by the heart when it pushes blood out into the arteries. This force is expressed in two numbers, such as 140/70. The first number is the systolic pressure—the amount of force used when the heart beats (contracts). The second number is the diastolic pressure—the force exerted when the heart is resting between beats.

Ordinarily, an adult's blood pressure is considered normal when the systolic reading is lower than 140 and the diastolic reading lower than 85–90. By these standards, there are an estimated 50 million Americans with high blood pressure, a number that includes people whose blood pressure registers normal because they are taking antihypertensive medication.

Before middle age, high blood pressure is more common among men than among women. Then the ratio reverses, suggesting that the female SEX HORMONES estrogen and progesterone play a role in protecting younger women against high blood pressure.

This assumption is supported by the behavior of a woman's BLOOD VESSELS during PREGNANCY. Soon after conception, a woman's body begins to secrete hormones that relax ligaments and muscles, including the smooth muscle in the walls of the uterus and the walls of the blood vessels. As a result, the uterus is able to expand to make room for the growing fetus, and blood vessels throughout the body may relax and dilate to grow wider, to accommodate an increased supply of blood for mother and baby—a process that may lead to the typical VARICOSE VEINS of pregnancy.

PERCENTAGE OF AMERICANS WITH HIGH BLOOD PRESSURE		
Age	Male	Female
18–24 yrs.	15.2%	3.5%
25–34	20.9	6.9
35–44	28.4	19.3
45–54	43.7	39.1
55–64	52.6	52.6
65–74	60.2	67.5

Source: *The Merck Manual*, 16th ed. (Rahway, NJ: Merck Research Laboratory, 1992), p. 416.

In the United States, high blood pressure is more common among African Americans than among whites, but regardless of age and race, women who develop hypertension generally fare better than men. In 1990, the death rates from high blood pressure were 6.1 per 100,000 white males; 29.6 per 100,000 for black males (29.6); 4.7 per 100,000 for white females; and 22.5 per 100,000 for black females.

hip   The gross anatomy of the hip bone and joint is the same in men and women, but the details are slightly different. Like the rest of the bones in his body, a man's hip bones are larger and denser than a woman's and they are set closer together. As a result, his legs come down straighter, allowing him to move forward in a straight line while WALKING. The female hip bone has a smaller, shallower cup-shaped depression, and the opening in the bone into which the top of the femur (thigh bone) fits to form the hip joint is smaller and triangular compared with the larger oval opening in the male hip bone.

In old age, the smaller female hip bone is particularly sensitive to damage from OSTEOPOROSIS. A broken hip resulting from a fall is more common among females, particularly among postmenopausal women, who experience a dramatic decrease in bone density following the drop in estrogen secretion at menopause plus an increased incidence of falls. Elderly men fall, too, of course, but their bones are larger, more dense, and thus less likely to break. Thirty-three percent of women but only 17 percent of men who live to be 90 will suffer a hip fracture.

hip dislocation   Dislocation of the hip among newborns occurs most often in breech births, when the hip joint is stressed as the infant begins to emerge from the womb feet first rather than head first. This occurs equally among boys and girls. A second form of dislocation, displacement due to insufficient tension in the ligaments around the joint, occurs about once in every 1,500 births, six times more frequently among girls than among boys.

HIV (human immunodeficiency virus) infections   HIV attacks the cells of the IMMUNE SYSTEM, depressing immune functions and leaving the body open to a plethora of diseases and conditions from pneumonia to cancer. The best-known consequence of HIV infection is AIDS (ACQUIRED IMMUNE DEFICIENCY SYNDROME).

HIV is transmitted through intimate contact with body fluids. Men are most likely to acquire HIV through unprotected homosexual intercourse or through sharing needles for intravenous drug use. Among women, the leading source of infection is unprotected heterosexual intercourse. Both men and women transmit the HIV virus in body fluids—blood, semen, vaginal and cervical secretions—but males seem more likely to transmit the virus. For people having heterosexual intercourse, the risk of acquiring HIV from an infected male partner is 18 times higher than the risk of acquiring it from an infected female partner.

While both men and women can pass HIV on to a sexual partner, only a pregnant woman can transmit it directly to the fetus. Every baby born to a woman carrying the HIV virus will carry antibodies to the virus in its blood, but only an estimated 7 percent to 40 percent of these infants are actually infected with HIV. In July 1994, the Food and Drug Administration approved the use of zidovudine (AZT) for pregnant women to prevent them from passing the HIV virus to the fetus. In a randomized, double-blind trial (a study in which neither the researchers nor the participants know who is getting the drug and who is getting the placebo), HIV-infected pregnant women took 500 mg of AZT a day by mouth between their 14th and 34th weeks of pregnancy and were given the drug intravenously during labor. Slightly more than 25 percent of the women who did not get AZT passed the HIV virus on to their babies; among women who got AZT, the transmission rate was only 8 percent.

REPORTED DEATHS FROM HIV INFECTIONS, 1991

Age	Male	Female
All ages (yrs.)	26,046	*
1–14	137	122
15–34	8,661	1,440
35–54	15,372	1,615
55–74	*	*
75+	*	*

*HIV infections do not rank among the top ten leading causes of death in this age group.

Source: National Center for Health Statistics, *Vital Statistics of the United States, 1991* (Washington, D.C.: Public Health Service, 1994).

ESTIMATED DEATHS FROM HIV INFECTION, 1992

Age	Male	Female
0–14 yrs.	140	190
15–24	340	140
25–34	8,570	1,340
35–44	12,640	1,860
45–54	5,400	440
55+	2,280	240

Source: U.S. Centers for Disease Control, "Provisional numbers of deaths for the 10 leading causes of death by age, race and sex, United States, 1992," *Monthly Vital Statistics*, September 28, 1993.

Hodgkin's disease   Hodgkin's disease, a cancer of the lymph system, occurs approximately twice as frequently among men; in childhood, more than 80 percent of all Hodgkin's patients are boys. This has led some researchers to wonder whether susceptibility to Hodgkin's disease is influenced by male hormones or is an X-LINKED TRAIT carried in a gene on the X chromosome.

homicide victims   Overall, homicide is the tenth leading cause of death in the United States. Among young people, the toll is devastating. In 1991, the latest year for which complete numbers are available, homicide was the fourth leading cause of death among boys and girls younger than 14. It was the second leading cause of death among males age 15 to 34 and the third leading cause among females in the same age group. Among adults age 35 to 44, it was the seventh leading cause of death for males and the tenth leading cause of death for females.

REPORTED HOMICIDES, 1991

Age	Male	Female
All ages	20,768	*
1–14 yrs.	572	375
15–34	13,122	2,838
35–54	5,185	1,498
55–74	*	*
75+	*	*

*Homicide is not among the ten leading causes of death in this group.

Source: National Center for Health Statistics, *Vital Statistics of the United States, 1991* (Washington, D.C.: Public Health Service, 1994).

ESTIMATED DEATHS FROM HOMICIDE, 1992

Age	Male	Female
Less than 1 yr.	230	120
1–14	610	340
15–24	6,880	1,340
25–34	6,180	1,430
35–44	3,890	1,110
45–54	1,610	470
55–64	850	280
65–74	440	170
75–84	190	250
85+	40	60

Source: U.S. Centers for Disease Control, "Provisional numbers of deaths for the 10 leading causes of death by age, race and sex, United States, 1992," *Monthly Vital Statistics*, September 28, 1993.

The estimated death totals for 1992 showed a worsening trend, with a frightening new increase in the number of homicides among young women.

homosexuals, number of males versus females   In his pioneering studies of sex and sexuality in the United States in the 1940s and 1950s, Alfred Kinsey, author of *Sexual Behavior in the Human Male* and *Sexual Behavior in the Human Female*, estimated that as many as 37 percent of American men had had at least some homosexual experiences and 4 percent were exclusively homosexual from adolescence on. Among women, an estimated 13 percent of those interviewed had at least some homosexual experience, and 1 percent to 3 percent were exclusively homosexual throughout their lives. More recent research suggests

HOMICIDES INVOLVING GUNS, 1990

Age	Male	Female
Under 5	39	30
5–14	218	103
15–24	5,046	633
25–44	6,672	1,279
45–64	1,334	369
65–74	197	85
75+	123	90

Source: *The World Almanac and Book of Facts*, 1994 (Mahwah, NJ: World Almanac, 1994).

that anywhere from 4 percent to 10 percent of American men and 2 percent to 4 percent of American women are exclusively homosexual.

But these numbers come with a caveat. Whether they are accurate depends completely on whether the people who were interviewed told the truth. Given the natural human tendency to inflate the reality of sexual performance or lie about behavior others might consider unusual, there is much justified suspicion about any estimates of the prevalence of homosexuality in the United States.

I

icthyosis   Icthyosis (from the Greek words for "fish" and "condition") is a group of inherited diseases that cause the skin to scale. The scaling may be fine and localized or may be thick and spread all over the body.

X-linked icthyosis, which causes large, dark scales that turn darker with age, is an X-LINKED TRAIT, transmitted via a gene on the X chromosome. It occurs once in every 6,000 births, and like other X-linked traits, including HEMOPHILIA and COLOR BLINDNESS, it affects males almost exclusively. To show the effects of this gene, a female must inherit it on an X chromosome from both her mother and her father.

immune system   The immune system is the body's primary defense against infection and disease. It disarms or destroys invading microbes, speeds healing, and prevents body cells from growing wildly, with no plan or pattern.

The working agents of the immune system are lymphocytes—white blood cells formed in lymphoid tissue. B cells, lymphocytes formed in the bone marrow, are short-lived cells responsible for the production of circulating immunoglobulins, proteins that act as antibodies. T cells, which also form in bone marrow but mature in the thymus, are long-lived (months to years) cells that affect immune response between cells. Null cells (also known as killer cells) are immune cells defined by the fact that they are neither T nor B. NK ("natural killer") cells are a subgroup of null cells. Phagocytes are white blood cells whose function is to swallow and inactivate invading microorganisms. Complement cells—enzymes in the blood that start the biological processes that protect the body against toxins—enhance the work of the T cells, B cells, null cells, and phagocytes.

The female immune system is superior even in the womb; more boys than girls are spontaneously aborted or are stillborn. Once born, males are more susceptible to bacterial and viral infections, and more contract and die of cancer. Clearly, their naturally lower resistance to pathogens or cellular changes is one reason why men do not live as long as women.

Why is a woman's immune system stronger than a man's? Perhaps natural selection has equipped women with protective genes that protect immune function. Genetic research shows that a number of the genes regulating the immune system are at home on the X chromosome. Many immune-system deficiencies are sex-linked characteristics that affect men more often and more severely than women. Finally, the female hormone estrogen appears to boost immune function, so that women seem to muster larger numbers of antibodies in response to specific challengers such as polio viruses and the E. coli bacteria that cause food poisoning.

That's the good news (for women). The bad news, says Rockefeller University rheumatologist Robert G. Lahita, is that "the female immune system is so finely tuned that it has a greater opportunity to go awry, and it often does." When that happens, a woman's immune functions are more likely to go overboard rather than cut back, to be hyperactive rather than inhibited. As a result, women are at higher risk of autoimmune conditions such as ARTHRITIS and Lupus in which the body attacks its own tissues.

immune system deficiency disorders, inherited   Approximately 70 percent of those with inherited deficiencies of the immune system are male, so it seems reasonable to assume that most of these disorders are X-LINKED TRAITS, carried on the X chromosome. Approximately half of immune system defects are B cell defects; defects of the T cells account for another 30 percent; deficiencies of phagocytes, 20 percent; defects in the complement cells, 2 percent.

infertility   About 14 percent of couples are infertile—unable to conceive after one year of intercourse without contraceptives. Infertility is equally common in men and women. Male factors are at work in 40 percent of all cases of infertility; female factors in 40 percent. In the remaining 20 percent, there is a combination of the two. What does differ is the reasons for male and female infertility, differences based on the differences in anatomical structures.

In men, infertility may be due to an abnormal sperm count resulting from a hormonal imbalance, exposure to various medical drugs, or environmental hazards such as lead or heat. Even if he produces a sufficient number of sperm, a man may be infertile if the sperm are not sufficiently mobile, or if they cannot

---

A SELECTED LIST OF COMMON MEDICAL DRUGS
THAT MAY AFFECT FERTILITY

1. Drugs that may inhibit sperm production:
   Anticancer drugs
   Antimalarial drugs
   Aspirin (chronic use)
   Colchicine
   Cortisone
   Male and female hormones
   Marijuana
   Metaclopramide
   Methotrexate
   Nitrofuradantoin
   Spirnolactone
   Sulfasalazine
   Urinary antiseptics
2. Drugs that reduce fertility by reducing ovarian function:
   Anesthetic gases
   Anticancer drugs
   Danazol
   Hormones (medroxyprogesterone)
3. Drugs that may cause impotence (failure to attain erection):
   Anticholinergics
   Antihistamines
   Antihypertensives
   Estrogens
   Mood altering drugs

Source: James W. Long and James J. Rybacki, *The Essential Guide to Prescription Drugs* (New York: HarperCollins, 1995); Physician's Desk Reference, 48th ed. (Montvale, N.J.; Medical Economics Production Company, 1994).

---

make their way to the penis because the approach ducts are deformed or scarred by infection, or if he cannot attain or sustain an erection or ejaculate.

A woman may be infertile if a hormonal imbalance prevents her from releasing a mature egg each month, or if the egg she releases cannot pass through fallopian tubes scarred by infection or blocked by implants of endometrial tissue (endometriosis), or if thick mucus at the cervix prevents the sperm from passing up into the uterus to meet the egg.

insomnia   Women complain of insomnia twice as frequently as men, and most sleep studies show more women reporting trouble getting to sleep. In a 1994 analysis of 43 previous surveys comparing sleep behavior in men and women, 16 of 21 studies reported women having more trouble falling asleep and staying asleep through the night; 14 of 17 studies showed that women are more likely to use drugs to get to sleep.

There is much circumstantial evidence to suggest that a woman's inability to fall asleep or stay asleep is due to her hormones. Kathryn Lee, a nurse researcher at the University of California investigating the possibility that sleep disturbances during pregnancy make women vulnerable to postpartum depression, recruited women planning to become pregnant and monitored their sleep patterns before pregnancy, through each of the three trimesters, and in the first few months after delivery.

She found that pregnant women do tend to spend more of the night lying awake in bed. Instead of writing this off as the result of simple physical discomfort, Lee proposes that sleep problems during pregnancy may be related to an increased level of progesterone, which is secreted in increasing amounts by the placenta as it grows during the first trimester. Ordinarily, progesterone is a relaxant, but the high levels present during pregnancy increase body temperature, quicken breathing, and loosen the smooth muscle of the uterus and bladder so that a pregnant woman feels a need to urinate more frequently, thus waking repeatedly during the night.

Hormones also play a part in the insomnia that many women experience at menopause, when the ovaries' secretion of estrogen slows, leading to recurring hot flashes that disrupt deep sleep.

A normal sleep pattern produces increasingly deeper sleep, with correspondingly slower brain waves. Several times a night, the sleeper rises to a lighter sleep with rapid eye movement (dreaming stage) and then sinks back down into deep sleep. Before menopause, healthy women customarily experience more restful sleep than light dreaming sleep, says sleep researcher Roseanne Armitage of the University of Texas. However, some studies show that women suffering from DEPRESSION or significant symptoms of PMS get only one-third as much deep sleep as women who do not experience significant mood swings. And, at menopause, recurring hot flashes caused by declining estrogen levels repeatedly bring women up from deep to light and less refreshing sleep that leaves them tired, disoriented, and possibly depressed the following day.

iron, dietary requirements   Iron is a trace element found in a number of enzymes essential to life. It is stored in red pigments in blood cells that carry oxygen to every cell and tissue in the body. There is one milligram of iron for every milliliter of red blood cells in your body. Because men have more red blood

IRON REQUIREMENTS

Age	RDA
Birth to 6 months	6 mg
6 months–10 years	10 mg
11–18 years	
males	12 mg
females	15 mg
19–50 years	
males	10 mg
females	15 mg
50+	10 mg

Source: National Research Council, *Recommended Dietary Allowances,* 10th ed. (Washington, D.C.: National Academy Press, 1989).

cells, they have more stored iron and are less susceptible to IRON DEFICIENCY ANEMIA.

The average man has approximately 30 milliliters (ml) of red blood cells/30 milligrams (mg) of iron for every kilogram (2.2 pounds) of body weight; the average woman, approximately 27 ml of red blood cells and 27 mg of iron. A 150-pound man has approximately 2,040 ml of packed red blood cells and 2,040 mg of iron, while a 150-pound woman has only about 1,840 mg of iron circulating in her blood.

Men also have more reliable blood stores of iron. In the United States, the average body store of iron is estimated to be approximately 1,000 mg for a man,

GOOD SOURCES OF IRON

Food Portions That Provide 25–39 Percent of the RDA for Adults and Children Older Than Four

Farina, cooked	2/3 cup
Oatmeal, instant	2/3 cup
Cereals, ready-to-eat	1 oz.
Beef liver, braised	3 oz.
Chicken or turkey, diced	½ cup
Oysters, baked, broiled, steamed, canned (drained)	3 oz.
Soybeans, cooked	½ cup

Source: *Good Sources of Nutrients* (Washington, D.C.: USDA, Human Nutrition Services, January 1990).

300 mg for a woman. Healthy adult men lose about 1 mg of iron each day. The average daily loss for a healthy adult woman is approximately 1.5 mg because of the additional loss of iron during menstrual bleeding.

To replace the iron lost each day, adult males require 14 micrograms (µg) of iron a day for every kilogram of body weight, or 1.3 mg a day. Healthy premenopausal adult women need 22 µg per kg body weight, about 1.8 mg. Because the body does not absorb all the iron it gets, their RDAs are significantly higher: 10 mg a day for men older than 15; 15 mg a day for women.

iron deficiency anemia   Iron deficiency anemia (too little iron in the blood) is generally the result of a slow, steady loss of blood. A sudden growth spurt at adolescence may produce a temporary iron deficiency in boys, but in men it is almost always due to bleeding from an internal lesion such as an ulcer or a gastrointestinal tumor. In women, the most common cause of iron deficiency anemia is the natural loss of blood while menstruating. Because menstruation is clearly more common than gastrointestinal tumors, there are always more anemic women than anemic men.*

But are they really anemic? As of now, "normal" iron levels are really normal iron levels for men. To insist that these are also normal for women is to label virtually all women of childbearing age anemic, which means "sick"—a judgment that flouts reality. In the past few years, medicine has come to recognize that a woman's body does not always behave like a man's, and that research based solely on what works for men may short-change women. In fact, there are new studies to suggest that high blood levels of iron may increase a person's risk of heart disease and some forms of cancer. If this turns out to be true, then female iron levels, lower than the male "norm," may be the more protective standards.

iron overload   Iron deficiency anemia is too little iron in the body; iron overload, too much. Most iron overload is due to hemochromatosis, a metabolic disorder of unknown origin that causes increased absorption of iron from the intestinal tract, creating iron deposits that may damage tissue in the liver, pancreas, heart, and pituitary gland.

Inherited hemochromatosis is a genetic defect carried as a recessive trait on an autosomal gene (a chromosome other than the sex-determining X or Y). Its symptoms include darkened skin color, diabetes mellitus, impaired heart and

---

*Although the absence of menstrual periods during pregnancy might be expected to raise a woman's iron levels, the fact is that pregnant women need iron supplements in order to meet the growing fetus's demand for iron.

liver function, arthritic joints, weakness, lassitude, loss of weight, pain in the abdomen, and a lack of libido due to a failure of gonad development.

About 5 percent of all whites of European Anglo-Saxon ancestry carry the gene for inherited hemochromatosis. A 1983 study of 30-to-39-year-old males in central Sweden found a gene frequency of 6.9 percent; a 1985 study in the United States, a 3.8 percent frequency. Iron overload is five to ten times more common in men, perhaps because women have naturally lower iron levels and periodically lose blood and iron during menstruation.

Iron overload may also occur among people who consume abnormally large amounts of iron over long periods of time. For example, iron overload was once common among members of the Bantu tribe in South Africa, who once consumed large amounts of beverages fermented in iron vessels that leeched iron into the liquid. The symptoms of diet-related hemochromatosis are similar to those of inherited hemochromatosis.

irritable bowel syndrome   Irritable bowel syndrome, also known as spastic colon, is a prime example of an emotion-triggered response. People with irritable bowel syndrome are generally in excellent health, but they have a highly sensitive gut that tightens under tension or rebels when they eat the "wrong" foods. The symptoms of irritable bowel syndrome include painful spasms, periodic constipation, or, paradoxically, diarrhea, as well as gas, bloating, and nausea. This syndrome is three times more common in women than in men.

J

jawbones Like all the other bones in his body, a man's jawbone is usually larger than a woman's, and his chin is square, while the female chin is generally rounded or pointed. These are two features that assist forensic experts in identifying the gender of a SKELETON.

jaw pain The temporomandibular joint is the hinge at the side of the face that allows the lower jaw to open and close. (The upper jaw is part of the skull and therefore stationary.) Like muscles in the shoulder, abdomen, hand, and back, the muscles that operate this joint are a TARGET AREA for stress-related tension that can cause temporomandibular joint disorder (TMD), excruciatingly painful spasms in the side of the face that are far more common in women than in men.

TMD may also be caused by clenching the jaw or grinding the teeth, or, more rarely, by degenerative arthritis in the joint or by chewing with poorly aligned teeth or badly fitted dentures.

K

Kaposi's sarcoma   Until the advent of AIDS, Kaposi's sarcoma was best known as a slow-growing tumor occurring mainly in people older than 60, usually men of Jewish or Italian ancestry. In 90 percent of the cases, Kaposi's sarcoma was essentially benign, characterized by slowly expanding bumps or ulcers on the leg that could be treated by simple surgery or radiation therapy.

The current, more aggressive form of Kaposi's sarcoma found in AIDS victims spreads through the lymph system to attack lymph nodes and organs, including the intestinal tract. Kaposi's sarcoma is still more common in men, especially in men with HIV infections. In 1995, researchers identified a virus associated with Kaposi's sarcoma in AIDS patients. It is not clear whether this virus actually causes the disease.

kidney cancer   Although the incidence of kidney cancer has been rising in both sexes, in the United States a man's risk is still nearly double a woman's.

In 1995, the American Cancer Society estimated 18,800 new cases of kidney cancer (17,100 men, 11,700 women) and an estimated 11,700 deaths (7,100 men, 4,600 women). Comparing the period between 1959 and 1961 with the period between 1989 and 1991 shows a 33 percent increase in deaths from kidney cancer among American men, from 3.9 to 5.2 deaths per 100,000. In the same time period, kidney cancer deaths rose 20 percent among American women, from 2.0 to 2.4 per 100,000. Today, the person most likely to develop kidney cancer is a man aged 50 to 60.

Because carcinogenic chemicals in tobacco smoke are eliminated through the kidneys and bladder, smoking is a risk factor for kidney cancer. Therefore, it's entirely possible that the current figures showing a higher incidence and death rate among men, like the figures for LUNG CANCER, may be skewed by the fact that more men smoke.

**AGE GROUPS IN WHICH KIDNEY DISEASE (NEPHRITIS)
WAS AMONG THE 10 LEADING CAUSES OF
REPORTED DEATHS, 1991**

Age	Male	Female
All ages	—	10,942
55–74	—	2,812
75+	6,078	—

Source: National Center for Health Statistics, *Vital Statistics of the United States, 1991* (Washington, D.C.: Public Health Service, 1994).

---

kidney infection   Like URINARY TRACT INFECTIONS, kidney infections, (also known as nephritis) are more common among women, whose shorter urethra (the urinary opening) is close to the anus and the vagina, allowing for bacteria to move more quietly into the bladder. In 1991, kidney infections were the ninth leading cause overall of reported deaths among American women.

kidney stones   Kidney stones are composed of crystals of calcium, uric acid, or struvite—uric acid that has been split by bacteria into magnesium ammonium phosphate, a solid material normally found in urine. Nearly 80 percent of kidney stones are made of calcium; approximately 8 percent are uric acid; the rest are struvite.

The person most likely to develop kidney stones is a man older than 30 whose relatives also have kidney stones. Men are two to three times more likely to develop calcium stones, and their risk of uric acid stones is significantly higher, because uric acid stones are more common among people with gout (which is nine times more common among men) or with a family history of stones. Women are more likely to produce struvite stones, because they are more likely to develop the urinary infections that provide the bacteria to create struvite.

L

language and speech   Language comprises the words we use and the rules that govern the way we put those words together to communicate with each other. Speech is the physical ability to utter sounds (words) so as to express thoughts; it requires muscle as well as brain power.

As a rule, girls master language and speech faster than boys do. Not only do girls begin to talk earlier; they talk more, and their verbal skills are superior for as long as they live. Until recently, most attempts to explain this gender difference have relied on anecdotal or cultural evidence such as the observation that new mothers talk more to their girl babies, who respond to the stimuli by talking more back to them.

But the difference may turn out to be physical. Early in 1989, a group of scientists specializing in the new field of gender-related difference in brain anatomy and function met at the New York Academy of Sciences to trade information. One important presentation was the report by Sandra Witelson of McMaster University in Hamilton, Ontario that the CORPUS CALLOSUM, a bridge between the brain hemispheres, is larger in the female brain than in the male, even though the male brain, like the male body, is generally larger overall.

Based on a study at autopsy of 15 male and 35 female patients, Witelson found that the isthmus, a narrow, bridgelike section at the rear of the corpus callosum, is larger in women than in men. The isthmus connects the verbal and spatial thinking centers of the left and right hemispheres.

In 1992, examining 14 brains at autopsy, Witelson reported finding a second part of the corpus callosum, the splenum, also larger in women. Like the isthmus, the splenum connection seems to influence verbal abilities. Using magnetic resonance imaging (MRI) to measure brain activity in 29 living women, scientists at the University of California–Los Angeles medical school found that the

84

larger the splenum, the better the women performed on verbal fluency tests, leading the researchers to theorize that the larger female splenum may provide an anatomical basis for the better female language skills through increased lines of communication between the left and right hemispheres that allow women to connect or shift functions back and forth between the hemispheres of the brain.

left-handedness   The preference for using one hand, most commonly the right rather than the left, is linked to the dominance of one side of the brain over the other. If the left side of the brain is dominant, the right hand leads; if the right side is dominant, the left hand is favored.

Ordinarily, the left side of the brain exerts more control. As a result, more than nine of every ten human beings are naturally right-handed, and probably right-footed, as well. A majority of the remaining 10 percent, the lefties, are male; some researchers suggest that gay men and lesbian women are less consistently right-handed than are heterosexual men and women.

There are several possible but unconfirmed explanations for left-handedness. Because a preference for one hand shows up early in life, usually well before a child enters school, it may be simply a recessive inherited trait. Or it may be the body's compromise when the right side of the brain is damaged before or soon after birth. Or it may be caused by unusual levels of the male SEX HORMONE testosterone—too low in men or too high in women—which may (or may not) explain the higher incidence of left-hand preference among gay men and lesbians.

A new, intriguing possibility is that left-handers may just be people with better communication between the two sides of the brain. According to Salk Institute biologist Simon LeVay, while the left side of the brain is dominant in language in about 95 percent of right-handed people, it is also dominant in up to 50 percent of left-handers, implying superior connections that allow conscious or unconscious switching of functions between the hemispheres. If this is true, it would not only explain left-hand preference, but why left-handed people seem to recover faster and more fully from a STROKE on the left side of the brain involving LANGUAGE AND SPEECH. [See also CORPUS CALLOSUM.]

legs   A man's legs are longer in proportion to his trunk than a woman's are in proportion to hers. This difference almost certainly arises from the longer male adolescent growth period, when the legs grow faster than the body [see GROWTH]. Longer legs and a relatively shorter trunk give men an advantage in speed running, high jump, and long jump. The fastest man to date, Carl Lewis, was clocked at 26 miles per hour in 1988 at the Olympic Games in South Korea.

WORLD RECORDS IN RUNNING

Event	Male min:sec	Female min:sec
100 meters	0:9.8	0:10.49
200 meters	0:19.72	0:21.34
1,000 meters	2:12.18	2:30.6
1 mile	3:46.32	4:15.61
2,000 meters	4:50.81	5:28.69
10,000 meters	26:58.38	30:13.74

Source: *The Guinness Book of Records, 1994* (New York: Bantam Books, 1993), p. 748, p. 750.

WORLD RECORDS IN JUMPING

Events	Men ft/in	Women ft/in
High jump	8'0"	6'10 ¼"
Long jump	29'4 ½"	24'8 ¼"

The Guinness Book of Records, 1994 (New York: Bantam Books, 1993), p. 749.

At the same Olympics, the fastest woman, Florence Griffith Joyner, only reached a running speed of 24.58 miles per hour.

leukemia   Most forms of leukemia occur at equal rates in men and women. One exception is chronic lymphocytic leukemia (CLL), a form of the disease in which white blood cells multiply wildly, circulating through the lymph nodes, the lymph tissue, and the blood, ultimately invading the bone marrow. CLL is three times more common among men than among women. A second exception is hairy cell leukemia, so named because the affected cells have hairlike threads coming off the surface. Hairy cell leukemia is a slow-moving disease characterized by a reduction in the number of red blood cells, white blood cells, and platelets, plus recurrent bacterial infections. It is most likely to strike in middle age; the ratio of men to women is five to one.

life expectancy   From the moment of conception, females are hardier than males. More boys are conceived and born, but they die at a faster clip. Around the world, while the numbers may vary, there are always more older women than older men. Women may outlive men by as much as seven years or more.

LIFE EXPECTANCY IN THE UNITED STATES

Year of Birth	Male (years)	Female (years)
1940	60.8	65.2
1950	65.6	71.1
1960	66.6	73.1
1970	67.1	74.7
1980	70.0	77.5
1990	71.8	78.8
1992	72.3	79.0

Source: *World Almanac and Book of Facts, 1994* (Mahwah, NJ: World Almanac, 1993), p. 972.

NUMBER OF AMERICANS OLDER THAN 65, 1990

Age	Male	Female
65+	12,497,766	18,586,129
80+	2,197,057	4,733,414
100+	8,000	32,000

Source: *World Almanac and Book of Facts, 1994* (Mahwah, NJ: World Almanac, 1993), p. 958.

In 1991, the country with the highest average life expectancy was Japan. There, a newborn baby girl could expect to live 82.1 years, a newborn baby boy, 76.1. In the United States, life expectancy is slightly lower—79 years for a girl and 72.3 years for a boy—and there are only 46 men for every 100 women older than 80.

Less than a quarter of the estimated 40,000 people worldwide who have passed the century mark are men. The oldest person in the world whose birth can reliably be documented is a woman, Jeanne Louise Calment. Mlle. Calment, who was born in France on February 21, 1875, was still alive 120 years later to celebrate her birthday in 1995. Her sense of humor was definitely intact. Asked by a reporter what kind of future she expected, she replied: "A short one."

lipoproteins   Lipoproteins are fat and protein molecules that carry CHOLES-TEROL around and out of the body. Low density lipoproteins (LDLs), the "bad" particles, are small and dense enough to carry cholesterol through the arterial membranes, contributing to the buildup of fatty plaque that causes coronary artery disease. High density lipoproteins (HDL), the "good" particles, are too large and fluffy to pass into the artery; they take cholesterol out of the body.

In childhood, boys and girls tend to have similar levels of lipoproteins. At puberty, levels of LDL particles rise and levels of HDL particles drop in both males and females. But owing to the influence of the sex hormones estrogen and testosterone, HDL levels remain higher in women; LDL levels stay higher in men. According to the long-running Framingham (Massachusetts) study that first identified high cholesterol levels as a risk factor for coronary artery disease, among adults age 25 to 50, 43.5 percent of the men versus 14.8 percent of the women have unfavorable HDL/LDL profiles. This difference is thought to explain why men are at higher risk for premature coronary artery disease. In addition, women's LDLs are larger and less likely to carry fats into their arteries.

At mid-life, when women approach menopause, things change once again. Now the secretion of estrogen slows; HDL levels drop and LDL levels rise, sometimes above those of men in the same age group. More women develop heart disease, but the incidence of the disease among women—that is, the number of cases for every 100,000 individuals—never quite equals the incidence among men. To the end, even with "unfavorable" ratios of lipoproteins, women maintain an edge.

liver   The liver is the largest gland in the body, a chemical factory that manufactures proteins (including the lipoproteins that carry fats around and out of the body); produces bile salts to digest and absorb fats; converts fats and proteins to carbohydrates; secretes enzymes that digest carbohydrates including ALCOHOL; stores carbohydrates as glycogen that provides energy directly to body cells; breaks amino acids, the building blocks of proteins, into nitrogen that can be excreted from the body in urine; serves as the body's poison control center, detoxifying harmful substances and metabolizing drugs; and plays a major role in the birth and death of blood cells.

The liver also inactivates and modifies hormones, including the SEX HORMONES estrogen and testosterone. As a result, there are specific gender influences on liver function.

The female liver produces smaller amounts of an enzyme, alcohol dehydrogenase, needed to metabolize alcoholic beverages. In addition, the female hormone estrogen may inhibit the liver's processing of bilirubin, the yellow-gold waste product created when red blood cells are destroyed at the natural end of their four-month life cycle or through disease. If this happens, there will be an increase in the amount of bilirubin circulating through the small blood vessels just under the surface of the skin, adding a dusky golden cast called jaundice (from *jaune*, the French word for yellow). This is fairly common in the third trimester of pregnancy, when naturally higher levels of estrogen can cause a temporary yellowing of the skin ("pregnancy jaundice").

As for the male hormone testosterone, any change in the liver's ability to metabolize the hormone may lead to a thinning of the pubic hair and the hair under the arms, as well as enlarged breasts and atrophy of the testicles. This often occurs in CIRRHOSIS OF THE LIVER, which is more common among men.

liver cancer   In 1995, the American Cancer Society estimated 9,800 new cases of liver cancer and 7,700 deaths among men in the United States; 8,700 new cases and 6,500 deaths among women. Liver cancer is the ninth leading cause of cancer death among men, and the eighth leading cause of cancer death among women. Women using birth control pills have an increased risk of benign liver tumors, but reducing the amount of estrogen in the pill has lowered the incidence of these tumors.

lung cancer   In 1995, the American Cancer Society estimated lung cancer to be the leading cause of cancer death in the United States, with 96,000 new cases and 95,400 deaths among American men; 73,900 new cases and 62,000 deaths among American women.

According to the American Lung Association, lung cancer and other forms of lung disease are more prevalent among men because more men have smoked for longer periods of time and because more men work with chemicals and pollutants in situations where there is what ACS calls a "careless disregard" of workers' health and "callous flouting" of clean air laws.

In 1990, ACS statistics showed that approximately 16,300 lung cancer deaths could be blamed directly on exposure to ionizing radiation or inhalation of carcinogens in the factory/manufacturing workplace such as asbestos, arsenic, chloroethers, chromates, nickel, and polynuclear aromatic hydrocarbons. Therefore, as women smoke and move into chemical manufacturing jobs that were

CHANGES IN THE INCIDENCE OF LUNG CANCER PER 100,000 PEOPLE, 1980–1986

	1980	1986	% change
Black males	131.6	130.2	-1.1
White males	82.4	80.2	-2.7
Black females	34.9	43.3	+24.1
White females	28.4	37.2	+30.9

Source: American Lung Association, *Lung Disease Data 1993*.

once exclusively male, there is likely to be an increasing balance between the sexes.

In recent years, the incidence and rate of increase in lung cancer cases has fallen slightly among men, while soaring among women. Between 1976 and 1991, the number of lung cancer deaths among men rose 121 percent; among women, it went up 425 percent.

lungs   At birth, a newborn girl's lungs are usually larger and better developed than a newborn boy's. Because more boys than girls are either born prematurely or have respiratory difficulties, they are also more likely to succumb to bacterial infections of the lung that account for up to 38 percent of all deaths the first month of life among low birth weight infants or infants with respiratory problems. Premature boys are also more likely than premature girls to develop hyaline membrane disease [see FETUS].

In the course of a single day, an average adult, male or female, will breathe in 8,000 to 9,000 liters of air, aerating 8,000 to 10,600 liters (8,500–10,600 gallons) of blood that circulates through the heart to the pulmonary artery, on to the lungs and then back through the pulmonary vein to the heart, which pumps it out into the body. The size of an adult's lungs and how much blood they aerate in a single day depends on the size of the body. As a rule, adult male lungs are larger than adult female lungs.

M

macular degeneration   Macular degeneration is the leading cause of permanent vision loss in the elderly. It is a progressive but moderate loss of central vision due to atrophy and degeneration of a part of the retina known as Bruch's membrane. Ordinarily, both eyes are affected over a period of several years. People with macular degeneration can get around well although they have difficulty reading. Some analyses show macular degeneration to be more common in women; others show no difference between the sexes.

magnesium   Magnesium is essential for biochemical and physiological processes including the synthesis of tissues, the activation of more than 300 enzymes, the transmission of impulses from nerves to muscles, and the transport of nutrients across cell membranes.

Human magnesium requirements are based on body weight—approximately 4.5 mg magnesium is needed for each 2.2 pounds. The recommended daily dietary allowance for a healthy adult man of average weight (174 pounds) is 350 mg. The allowance for a healthy adult woman of average weight (139 pounds) is 280 mg. The RDA for pregnant women is 320 mg. According to the USDA Human Nutrition Information Service, adult American women generally get 74 percent of the RDA from their diet; adult American men, 94 percent.

Meeting the magnesium requirement is particularly important during pregnancy. Approximately 25 percent of the children diagnosed with cerebral palsy each year in the United States are very low birth weight infants. In 1995, Karin B. Nelson of the National Institute of Neurological Disorders and Stroke in Bethesda, Maryland and Judith K. Grether of the California Birth Defects Monitoring Program in Emeryville reported that giving magnesium supplements to women with problem pregnancies who were at risk of delivering low birth weight infants appears to reduce the risk of cerebral palsy.

RECOMMENDED DAILY DIETARY ALLOWANCES FOR MAGNESIUM

Age	RDA
Birth to 6 months	40 mg
6 months–1 year	60 mg
1–3 years	80 mg
4–6 years	120 mg
7–10 years	170 mg
11–14 years	
males	270 mg
females	280 mg
15–18 years	
males	400 mg
females	300 mg
19+	
males	350 mg
females	280 mg
Pregnant	320 mg
Lactating	
1st 6 months	355 mg
2nd 6 months	340 mg

Source: National Research Council, *Recommended Dietary Allowances*, 10th ed. (Washington, D.C., National Academy of Sciences, 1989).

GOOD SOURCES OF MAGNESIUM

Food Portions That Provide 10–24 Percent of the RDA for Adults and Children Older Than Four

Whole wheat bread	2 slices
Bran muffin	1 medium
Spaghetti, high protein, cooked	1 cup
Lima beans, cooked	½ cup
Broccoli, cooked	½ cup
Oysters, cooked	3 ounces
Scallops, cooked	3 ounces
Tofu, cubed	½ cup
Nuts and seeds	2 tablespoons
Milk, skim	1 cup
Yogurt, lowfat	1 cup

Source: *Good Sources of Nutrients* (Washington, D.C.: USDA, Human Nutrition Services, January 1990).

The report was based on a retrospective comparison of the prenatal treatment for 117 women who had given birth to children weighing less than 3.3 pounds. More than one-third of the women who bore healthy infants had taken magnesium to prevent convulsions related to pregnancy-induced high blood pressure. Among the women whose babies developed cerebral palsy, only 10 percent had taken magnesium. Nelson and Grether declined to theorize as to the link between the nutrient and the risk of cerebral palsy; earlier studies suggest the possibility that the mineral may prevent cerebral bleeding.

Marfan's syndrome   A BIRTH DEFECT, Marfan's syndrome is an inherited disorder of the connective tissue that results in disproportionately long fingers and toes, arms whose span may actually exceed a person's height, joints that are flexible enough to bend backward as well as forward, and deformities of eyes and heart. Marfan's syndrome is caused by a single gene; it is more common among children born to older fathers.

marriage   Single women have a better chance than their married sisters of celebrating a 100th birthday, but married men are much more likely than bachelors to live to a ripe old age.

In 1990, when they released the results of a ten-year survey of 1,011 men age 45 to 54, University of California–San Francisco researchers reported a higher death rate among unmarried men. Twenty-three percent of the men who lived alone or with a family, a "significant other," or some other unrelated person had died, versus 10.6 percent of those who were married and living with their wives.

This echoes the results of an earlier (1971–1975) study from the National Center for Health Statistics (NCHS)—a survey of 7,651 American adults designed to assess the impact of an adult's living arrangements on his or her longevity. After taking into account differences in income and education and such "hazardous" or "healthful" factors as smoking, drinking, weight, and physical activity, the researchers found that marriage is definitely a lifesaver for men age 45 to 64. Men who lived alone or in an unmarried relationship were twice as likely to die within ten years as were married men living with their wives.

Middle-aged women, 45 to 54, living with someone other than a spouse, were also at higher risk of early death, but after age 54, the death rate for married and single women was exactly the same. Those who lived alone or with a person other than a spouse were not at higher risk unless they were in a low-income group.

mathematical skills   Like the female facility with words [see LANGUAGE AND SPEECH], the male talent for numbers is something most people take for granted, and in fact, despite all attempts to even the academic playing field between the sexes, on average boys still seem to do better on math tests and tests of SPATIAL REASONING.

The use of modern imaging techniques has made it possible to detect and evaluate differences in the way male and female brains work, including the way they work out a mathematical problem.

One example of the new techniques is positron emission tomography (PET scan), which records changes in electrical charge to show living tissue at work, including the tissue of the brain. In 1994, Richard Haier, professor of pediatrics and neurology at the University of California–Irvine, obtained PET scans of 44 students (22 men, 22 women) who volunteered to have their brain activity recorded while they were doing SAT math problems. Half of the students (male and female) were superior mathematicians, with SAT scores higher than 700; the other half had average math skills, with SAT scores around 540.

Haier's PET scans showed distinctly different patterns of activity in male and female brains. While the high-scoring males were doing math problems, the activity in their temporal lobe (an area of the brain right behind the ear) was greater than in the men with average math ability. But the brighter women had very little activity in the temporal lobe, a pattern similar to the level of brain activity in the average female students.

The bright men and the bright women ended up doing equally well, but the PET scans suggest that they used different parts of their brains to get there. This is similar to the results of studies at Yale University using MRI images to capture pictures of the male and female brain READING or evaluating EMOTIONS.

measles   Boys get measles at about the same rate as girls do, but one potential long-term complication is more common among males.

Subacute sclerosing panencephalitis (SSPE) is a progressive, usually fatal brain disorder that may show up anywhere from several months to many years after an attack of measles. SSPE can cause diminished intellectual performance, memory lapses, temper tantrums, insomnia, and hallucinations, as well as muscle spasms, difficulty in swallowing, seizures, and atrophy of the optic nerve leading to blindness. It is usually fatal within one to three years.

While the cause is unknown, some suspect that the culprit is a naturally acquired altered measles virus. SSPE has been reported in children who got measles vaccine but did not have measles. Based on figures describing the nationwide patterns of measles vaccinations, there is an estimated one case of

SSPE for every one million doses of vaccine. This is much lower than the number of cases (6 to 22 per million) linked to measles itself.

Meniere's syndrome   Meniere's syndrome is a relatively uncommon condition whose symptoms include vertigo (a sensation of whirling or spinning even when one is standing still) and difficulty in maintaining balance. It may be linked to an increase in fluid in the inner ear affecting both hearing and balance. Meniere's syndrome was originally called "watchmaker's disease" because it was so common among those doing fine work requiring long periods of great concentration and hand control. Today, the condition seems to occur more frequently in women than in men.

migraine   Beginning in adolescence, women are three times more likely than men to suffer from classic migraine, the HEADACHE sometimes heralded by an "aura" effect of wavy lights.

Approximately 66 percent of women who suffer from migraine headaches get them most frequently at times when their hormones are in flux, such as right before menstrual bleeding begins, or while they are taking estrogens as medication—for example, in birth control pills. Many women with migraine experience a partial or complete remission at menopause, which suggests (but does not prove) a link to estrogen. If estrogen really is the culprit, there is still no clear explanation of the mechanism by which it exerts its influence.

Cluster headache, a form of migraine characterized by several headaches a day for several weeks or months and then none at all for weeks, months, or even years, is more common in men.

miscarriage (spontaneous abortion)   As many as 20 percent of all pregnancies end in miscarriage. Up to 85 percent of all miscarriages occur in the first three months of pregnancy; most appear to be caused by the body's rejecting a fetus with potentially fatal physical deformities or chromosomal defects.

More males are conceived, and thus more males are spontaneously aborted. In the first trimester, during the second month of pregnancy, there are approximately 431 males for every 100 females miscarried. In the fourth month of pregnancy, just at the beginning of the second trimester, the number is 281 males for every 100 females.

motion sickness   Motion sickness is not a sickness; it is a completely normal reaction that occurs any time people are exposed to excessive motion, round and round or up and down. Even astronauts get motion sickness, but when they do it has a fancier name: "space adaptation syndrome."

Motion sickness originates in the part of the brain that controls nausea and vomiting. How much movement it takes to set off the response varies from person to person, but it is well known that women generally tend to react sooner than men. This gender difference has not yet been explained, nor has the fact that children younger than two appear to be immune or that older people react less severely.

It is easier to prevent motion sickness than to cure it once it starts. Some travelers benefit from wearing a transdermal patch that delivers antinausea medication through the skin in continuous doses over a three-day period. Simple home remedies also help. For example, susceptible people often feel better when they sit in the middle of a ship or over the wings of an airplane where there is the least motion, or in the front seat of a car so they can focus on the horizon. It also helps to have a continual supply of fresh air, and to eat and drink very little before and during a trip.

multiple sclerosis   Multiple sclerosis (MS) is a slowly progressive disease that destroys myelin, the fat and protein covering on a nerve cell fiber that allows the cell to transmit messages to muscles. When the myelin cover is destroyed, the cell cannot send impulses to the contractile cells that control muscle movement. The body slowly loses the ability to use its muscles.

Women develop MS more frequently than men. According to the National Multiple Sclerosis Society, more than 70 percent of MS patients are female. There is, as yet, no explanation for this gender difference.

muscle   There are three types of muscle tissue: skeletal muscle, the smooth muscle of the internal organs, and the specialized muscle of the heart.

Skeletal muscle is also known as striated muscle or voluntary muscle, because of the striations (raised vertical strips) on the muscle fiber and because these muscles can be voluntarily controlled. Human beings have more than 600 different skeletal muscles, attached either directly to bones or to tendons attached to bones, skeletal muscles work in pairs. For example, when you bend your arm up at the elbow, the inside muscle contracts, while the outside one stretches to allow the movement.

Smooth muscle, which lacks striations, is also known as involuntary muscle. It controls the internal organs, causing the uterus to contract at orgasm or during childbirth, moving food through the intestines, and pushing blood through the veins. Heart muscle has some striations but less connective tissue than skeletal muscle.

Because the male SEX HORMONE testosterone favors the growth of muscle mass, pound for pound the male body is more muscular than the female. The difference begins with the surge of testosterone in adolescence that produces the typically male biceps, shoulder, and thigh muscles. As adults, men and women have different muscle-to-fat ratios, the man's higher than the woman's. No woman, regardless of how diligently she exercises, can ever produce muscle bulk equal to that of a man of similar size and weight.

The obvious consequence of a more muscular body is greater physical strength, but there are other, more subtle effects. Muscle stores less energy than fat and burns energy at a faster rate; a man's BASAL METABOLISM is higher than a woman's. Because muscle tissue contains more water, men can consume larger amounts of ALCOHOL without showing ill effects.

muscular dystrophy   Muscular dystrophies are inherited disorders that lead to progressive weakening and wasting of the muscles that control body movement. The two most prevalent forms of the disease are X-LINKED TRAITS—inherited defects transmitted via recessive genes on the X chromosome.

Duchenne muscular dystrophy occurs only among males. It appears early in childhood, between ages three and seven. A female carrier can pass the gene for Duchenne on to both sons and daughters, but only the sons will develop the disorder. As many as one-third of all boys born with Duchenne muscular dystrophy have no Duchenne relatives; their illness may be caused by a spontaneous mutation rather than an inherited defect. Becker's muscular dystrophy is less severe than Duchenne. It occurs only one-tenth as often, and shows up slightly later in life, between ages five and 15.

Boys born with Duchenne muscular dystrophy rarely live into adulthood, so they do not pass the gene along. Boys with Becker's muscular dystrophy may live long enough to have children. As with all sex-linked characteristics, if the father has Becker's but the mother is not a carrier, the sons will be unaffected; the daughters, with one X chromosome from the father, will be carriers. If these carrier daughters have sons, there is a 50 percent chance that the boys will inherit an X chromosome with the Becker's gene and develop muscular dystrophy.

myasthenia gravis   People with myasthenia gravis have a decreased number of receptors for acetylcholine, a chemical that allows nerves to transmit impulses to the muscles. The decrease is evident on cranial nerves, the nerves that emerge from the brain rather than the spinal cord and control movement and sensation in the ears, eyes, nose, tongue, face, throat, heart, lungs, stomach, and abdominal organs.

Myasthenia gravis strikes one person in every 1,000. Early in life, more girls than boys are affected. This pattern continues, with an average three female patients for every two males at every age. In women, myasthenia gravis appears most often between ages 20 and 40; in men, between ages 50 and 60.

N

neck   The neck is the top of the spinal column—a supporting pillar of seven vertebrae plus cartilage, wrapped in seven skeletal MUSCLES: the cricothyroid, scalenus medius, sternocleidomastoid, sternohyoid, omohyoid, thyrohyoid, and trapezius.

Because of the muscle-building influence of testosterone, a man's neck is proportionately larger and bulkier than a woman's. Occasionally, the thickness is striking enough to merit the description "bull neck," and sleep scientists suggest that this may be one explanation for the higher incidence of SLEEP APNEA among men.

But the quintessential gender difference between a male and a female neck is the bump in the front—a V-shaped cartilaginous structure at about the level of the fifth cervical vertebra with an angle that points forward further in men than in women.

This protuberance is the thyroid eminence, also known as the *promenentia laryngea*, the *protuberentia laryngea*, or, more familiarly, the Adam's apple. Myth says that it was caused by Adam's eating that fatal apple, which remained stuck forever halfway down his gullet. Not true, of course. The Adam's apple is a secondary male sex characteristic that appears at puberty when the male larynx enlarges and the male VOICE cracks just about the time that penis development ends.

And that is why Eve doesn't have an Adam's apple.

nightmares   Nightmares and night terrors occur during rapid eye movement (REM) sleep, when the muscles are relaxed but brain waves show patterns of mental alertness. During REM sleep we breathe more rapidly, our pulse quickens, and males (infants as well as adults) are likely to experience erection.

99

Most nightmares occur in the last cycle of sleep, right before awakening; night terrors, in the first sleep cycle. Both adults and children experience nightmares; night terrors are most common before the age of ten. A child caught in night terrors may cry or scream or display panic reactions such as perspiration and dilated pupils. Like other forms of sleep disorder such as SLEEP APNEA and SNORING, nightmares and night terrors are more common among boys.

O

obesity The medical definition of obesity is any weight 20 percent or more above what is considered "desirable" for a person's age and build. According to the National Academy of Science's Institute of Medicine, 35 percent of all American women and 31 percent of all American men may currently be described as obese. Because a woman's BODY COMPOSITION tends naturally toward a higher proportion of fat and a lower proportion of muscle, while a man's is exactly the opposite, it is not surprising to find more overweight women than overweight men at every age, and in every racial and ethnic group.

The problem is figuring out exactly what constitutes "desirable" weights in a country whose citizens come from every corner of the globe, with every different body type. The drawings of male and female figures used to illustrate American weight charts usually depict bodies with wide shoulders (male), small bust and waist (female); narrow hips, long arms and legs (male and female). In other words, the standard Northern European body type.

OVERWEIGHT AMERICANS		
Race	**Males** (% obese)	**Females** (% obese)
White	24.4%	25.1%
Black	25.7	43.8
Puerto Rican	25.2	37.3
Cuban American	29.4	34.1
Mexican American	29.6	39.1
Native American	33.7	40.3
Native Hawaiian	65.5	62.6

Source: *Heart and Stroke Facts, 1994 supplement* (Dallas: American Heart Association, 1994).

But are these shapes the correct models for predicting health and mortality for those with very different but wholly normal body types—short, stocky Eastern Europeans; tall, slim Kenyans; short, slight Asians; or West Africans with ample breasts and buttocks? In fact, modern weight charts still do not give adequate attention to the variety in American body shapes, especially those that conflict with current cultural ideals.

oral cancers   In 1995, the American Cancer Society estimated 28,150 new cases of oral cancer (cancer of the tongue, mouth, and esophagus) and 8,370 deaths. Overall, oral cancers are twice as common among men; they occur most often in men older than 40. Given the fact that smoking and heavy consumption of alcohol are known risk factors for oral cancer, it is reasonable to think that behavior, rather than genetics, is responsible for the higher number of cases among men. As with cancer of the esophagus, lung, kidney, and bladder, the increase in the number of women who smoke for long periods of time is likely to tilt us toward an unfortunate equality between the sexes.

organ transplants   The IMMUNE SYSTEM protects our bodies from foreign invaders—viruses, bacteria, and other microorganisms. That's good. Unfortunately, the immune system also attacks foreign tissues such as transplanted organs—a phenomenon called "rejection." That's not so good.

Scientists have known for years that the male body accepts organs from the female body more easily than the reverse. The culprit was believed to be a protein called H-Y manufactured in all male (but not female) cells—an antigen that stimulates a woman's body to produce antibodies, substances that attack and destroy antigens.

In 1995, an international research team from Great Britain, France, and the United States finally located the gene (called Smcy) responsible for the protein. It is located on the Y chromosome. A similar gene, called Smcx, was identified on the X chromosome.

Because men have one X chromosome and one Y chromosome, their bodies have both an Smcy and an Smcx gene. Their bodies produce—and can accept—both a "male" and a "female" version of the H-Y protein. But a woman has no Y chromosome. Her body does not manufacture the "male" H-Y protein and will attack if male tissue is transplanted into her body.

orgasm   Orgasm is the climax of SEXUAL AROUSAL. For men, orgasm (ejaculation) is most commonly produced by the friction of the penis moving against a surface such as the vaginal walls. For women, it may be triggered by manipulation of the clitoris or by movement of the penis inside the vagina.

The first step towards the male orgasm is a small discharge of semen (emission), followed by contractions of the prostate and urethra that create a sensation of ejaculation to come, something like the quick succession of breaths we take before we sneeze. Emission is controlled by the sympathetic nervous system. So are the contractions of small tubes in the testes that send seminal fluid up the sperm ducts, over the bladder and out into the urethra. As seminal fluid begins to flow, the bladder closes to prevent it from falling backwards. The semen moves through the prostate gland into the urethra and is propelled out into the vagina by the involuntary rhythmic contractions of ejaculation.

For women, orgasm creates contractions of the smooth muscle that controls the wall of the uterus and vagina. Some women are consciously aware of these contractions; others are not. At orgasm, some women develop a fleeting pink rash over the torso.

After orgasm, both men and women experience resolution, a general sense of well-being and emotional and physical relaxation. Biologically, resolution—which discourages movement away from the partner—may be nature's way of ensuring conception by giving the sperm time to reach the egg. However, contrary to folk myth, orgasm is not required in order for pregnancy to occur.

Following resolution, there is a period of time during which most men will be unable to achieve another erection and ejaculation. How long this lasts depends on age and physical condition. The younger the man, the quicker he is

---

Medications That May Inhibit Ejaculation
Antidepressants
Antihistamines
Antispasmodics
Diuretics
Female hormones
Muscle relaxants
Tranquilizers

Medications That Inhibit Female Orgasm
Antidepressants
Antihistamines
Antispasmodics
Diuretics
Muscle relaxants

Source: James W. Long and James J. Rybacki, *The Essential Guide to Prescription Drugs* (New York: HarperCollins, 1995).

---

able to repeat his sexual performance; teenage boys may be able to reach erection again within minutes after orgasm. Women do not experience a period of orgasmic incapacity; there is absolutely no physical reason why they cannot come to orgasm two or more times in quick succession.

The goal of simultaneous orgasm is an idea that actually echoes biological imperatives. During orgasm, the male pelvis thrusts forward, sending the penis deep into the vagina, to deliver sperm directly up against the cervix of the uterus. When a woman climaxes at the same time as her partner, the contractions of the vaginal walls help to keep sperm close to the cervix, thus increasing the possibility of conception. An added bonus of shared climax is a shared period of resolution and relaxation.

osteoporosis   Osteoporosis (literally, "bones full of holes") is a generalized loss of BONE that often leads to fractures. The female hormone estrogen protects bone density. Both men and women secrete estrogen, but women secrete more of it, and when their ovaries cease producing estrogen at menopause, their body levels of the hormone decline more precipitously. This faster, more sudden and dramatic decline may account for the equally sudden and dramatic loss of bone density that makes osteoporosis so much more common among women.

There are two common kinds of osteoporosis among the elderly. The first, Type I osteoporosis, which occurs primarily but not exclusively in women, is due to a decline in the production of the female hormone estrogen. It shows up first between the ages of 51 and 75 and is more devastating in women than in men simply because the decline in estrogen production is more spectacular in a female than in a male body. Type I osteoporosis leads primarily to the loss of the trabecular bone (also known as cancellous bone) that composes the internal latticework of the spinal vertebrae and is found in the rounded ends of the long bones of the arms and legs. Women with Type I osteoporosis are prone to fractures or compression of the vertebrae that give them a round-shouldered look or rob them of height.

Type II osteoporosis, also known as senile osteoporosis, occurs mainly in people older than 70. It is a more gradual loss of bone, twice as common in women as in men. Type II osteoporosis affects both trabecular bone and cortical bone, the compact nontrabecular part of bones. People with Type II osteoporosis often suffer fractures of the spinal vertebrae, the top of the thigh bone, the long bones of the arm and leg, and the bones of the pelvis. While Type I osteoporosis is the direct result of a drop in estrogen secretion, Type II may be caused by an age-related reduction in the body's ability to synthesize vitamin D, which then leads to an inability to absorb calcium and a reduction in the body's estrogen level.

Given the estrogen link to both types of osteoporosis in older people, current wisdom dictates estrogen supplements for women beginning at menopause. Because estrogen is also linked to an increased risk of BREAST CANCER and cancer of the endometrium, some have suggested a short course of the hormone around the time of menopause, to protect bones without endangering the rest of the body.* But a 1993 study from the Boston University Arthritis Center for the first time cast serious doubt on the efficacy of this kind of short-term estrogen therapy.

The researchers began by measuring the bones of 670 Caucasian women in Framingham, Massachusetts, the home of the long-running Framingham Heart Study that first identified cholesterol as a risk in heart disease. They assessed the women's previous estrogen use and recorded any bone fractures as the years went by. In the end, it turned out that while taking estrogen for fewer than seven years might briefly slow the pace of bone loss, it conveyed no protective effect on bones at age 75. Women who took estrogen for seven to ten years did end up with about 3 percent more bone mass than women who never took the hormone, but that difference was not considered significant. The incidence of fractures among women using estrogen for short periods of time as against those who had never used the hormone was similar, although the nonusers were likely to have more broken bones in their 60s (which was precisely when most women took estrogen). The researchers concluded that in order to gain meaningful protection from osteoporosis, women with a family history or any other risk factors for osteoporosis may need to take hormone replacement for their entire post-menopausal life.

In a similar study of white women living in a retirement community in California, Elizabeth Barrett-Connor of the University of California–San Diego found that nothing (including whether or not a woman took estrogen) affected bone loss and osteoporosis more than the total number of a woman's reproductive years prior to menopause. The longer her reproductive life, and the more estrogen her body produced, the greater her protection against bone loss as she aged.

---

* Prescribing progestins along with estrogen lowers the risk of endometrial but not breast cancer.

P

pain   Pain is a warning triggered by messages sent from receptors throughout the body to nerve cells in the brain. It alerts the body to injury. The rare person born without a sense of pain is forever at risk of burned fingers, broken bones, and rotting teeth. Without pain, a person cannot avoid danger or perceive his own physical limitations.*

People who do not feel pain readily are said to have a higher "threshold" of pain. Women are commonly thought to feel pain less acutely than men, but much of the lore relating to women's greater tolerance for pain is based on their ability to survive childbirth. Modern research shows that nature does appear to arm an expectant mother for delivery. During pregnancy, cravings for salty, fat, or sweet foods may be linked to the ability of these foods to facilitate the production of the neurotransmitter serotonin, a chemical that stimulates smooth muscle, such as the muscle of the uterus, and promotes a feeling of well-being. As a woman draws closer to term, her body begins to produce larger amounts of endorphins—naturally occurring, opiatelike chemicals that link up with brain receptors designed to hold painkilling drugs such as morphine. During labor and delivery, endorphin production rises; both animal and human placentas contain high levels of these natural painkillers.

Some studies show that more than one-third of those given placebos to ease pain report significant relief. Pain seems more intense when we are tired, anxious, or worried about more pain in the future; pain is less intense when we are distracted. People who hurt themselves while engaged in strenuous physical activity may not even feel the injury until they stop.

---

* Some physical conditions and diseases, such as leprosy, damage nerves and inhibit the ability to perceive pain.

pancreatic cancer   In 1995, the American Cancer Society estimated 24,000 new cases of pancreatic cancer and 27,000 deaths. The proportionately high number of deaths is due to the fact that there is no effective treatment for this disease.

Researchers at the University of Texas Southwestern Medical Center have succeeded in defining the initial changes that lead to tumors in hamsters that are similar to pancreatic cancerous tumors in human beings, and they have identified three factors that may increase the incidence and size of these tumors. The first is orotic acid, a nutrient found in dairy products. The second is a diet high in fat and protein. The third is the female sex hormone estrogen. How estrogen influences the growth of pancreatic tumors remains unclear. One possibility is that female hormones keep damaged cells alive and reproducing, so that a cell with mutated DNA survives and adds to the tumor mass. As of now, estrogen is considered the most significant promoter of pancreatic tumors in women.

In the United States, a man's risk of pancreatic cancer is about one-third higher than a woman's. Smoking is considered a risk factor for pancreatic cancer, so the currently higher male incidence of pancreatic cancer, like the higher male incidence of ORAL CANCER, esophageal cancer, LUNG CANCER, KIDNEY CANCER, and BLADDER CANCER, may be due to the fact that more men smoke. Since the early 1970s, when the number of male SMOKERS began to decline, the incidence of pancreatic cancer among men has gone down.

pelvis   Overall, the female pelvis is shallower and broader than the male, to accommodate an expanding uterus during pregnancy. The joint between the two pubic bones is longer in the female pelvis, and the pubic structure is more rectangular compared with the more triangular male structure. Where the lower part of the male pubic bone is convex, the female is concave, to allow a child's head and body to pass through more easily at birth.

At the outer perimeter of the pelvis, the female HIP bone is smaller, with a more triangular opening where the ball top of the femur (thigh bone) fits in, compared with a more oval opening in the male hip. In addition, the female hip has a cup-shaped, smaller and shallower depression on the hip bone. Finally, the female pelvic bones are more likely to exhibit small pits or scars resulting from childbirth, although some male pelvic bones also show pitting and scarring.

These gender differences in the structure of the pelvis are so clear that forensic scientists view the pelvis as the single most useful guide to determining the gender of an unidentified SKELETON.

perspiration   Perspiration is nature's air conditioner. As the body heats up, either during exercise or in response to rising temperatures, eccrine sweat glands all over the body, particularly on the face, the palms of the hands, the soles of the feet, under the arms, and in the groin secrete moisture that evaporates on the skin, temporarily lowering body temperature. Because they have a higher metabolic rate, men normally generate more body heat than women do, and thus perspire more copiously. This reaction is facilitated by testosterone, the male hormone. Estradiol, an estrogen, inhibits perspiration.

There are two kinds of sweat glands—eccrine glands and apocrine glands. Eccrine glands, which are found all over the body, respond to emotional stimulation as well as to heat. The response to heat, however, takes longer than the response to emotional triggers, which is virtually instantaneous. A normal, healthy adult produces about a liter of eccrine perspiration a day. Apocrine glands, found under the arms, in the groin, and around the nipples, secrete a scanty milky substance that is odorless at first but turns smelly when attacked by bacteria.

Men perspire most heavily from eccrine glands on their upper chest and back. Women perspire most heavily from apocrine glands under their arms. In both sexes, underarm perspiration carries a complex mixture of volatile chemicals, some of which produce the characteristic human BODY ODOR. In 1990, chemist George Preti of the Monell Chemical Senses Center in Philadelphia identified the source of underarm odor as odorous acids with between six and eleven carbons. The main odorous component in the mixtures of acids is a methyl-branched hexenoic acid, precursors of which are associated with the water-soluble portion of apocrine gland secretions.

Deodorants contain antibacterial agents to kill bacteria that produce malodorous chemicals, plus fragrance to mask the odor. Antiperspirants contain aluminum salts, which make the skin swell slightly, closing pores and reducing the amount of perspiration on the skin.

physical strength   The classic wedge-shaped male body, with wide, muscular SHOULDERS, narrow HIPS, and long, muscular LEGS, is well adapted for lifting and pushing WEIGHT.

Although some women are stronger than some men, the average man's heavier BONES, bulkier MUSCLES, broader shoulders, and larger HEART and lungs make him physically stronger than the average woman. As a result, a weight-lifting contest between a man and woman of the same weight is no contest. With rare exceptions, the man can expect to make off with the prize every time.

HEAVY-LIFTING RECORDS AMONG MEN AND WOMEN
OF EQUAL WEIGHT

Body Weight	Event	Record Weight Lifted	
		Men	**Women**
114 lbs.	Snatch*	266.25 lbs.	192.75 lbs.
	Jerk*	342.75	253.5
148 lbs.	Snatch	352.75	216
	Jerk	442	286.5
181 lbs.	Snatch	403.25	242.5
	Jerk	496	314

Source: *The Guinness Book of Records* (New York: Bantam Books, 1994).

*As Michael Feulner of Gold's Gym in New York City explains, "jerk" and "snatch" are Olympic lifting events. In the first, the athlete lifts the barbell from the floor to shoulder height, pauses briefly, then lifts it above his/her head. In the second, the athlete lifts the barbell from the floor and raises it over his/her head in one sweeping motion.

---

pneumonia and influenza   Pneumonia and influenza together make up the sixth leading cause of death in the United States. Until the eighth and ninth decades of life, more males than females succumb to these respiratory diseases. The turnaround among the elderly does not necessarily represent an increased female susceptibility, however; more likely it is due simply to the fact that in old age there are fewer men than women, and thus more female than male deaths.

population   Although more boys than girls are conceived and born [see CONCEPTION AND BIRTH RATES], after that it's all downhill for the males.

REPORTED DEATHS FROM PNEUMONIA, 1991

Age	Male	Female
All ages (yrs.)	36,214	41,646
1–14	194	148
15–34	640	375
35–54	2,012	*
55–74	8,262	5,699
75+	24,768	33,971

*Pneumonia/influenza is not one of the ten leading causes of death in this age group.

Source: National Center for Health Statistics, *Vital Statistics of the United States, 1991* (Washington, D.C.: Public Health Service, 1994).

ESTIMATED DEATHS FROM PNEUMONIA/INFLUENZA, 1992		
Age	**Male**	**Female**
Less than 1 yr.	370	350
1–14	140	210
15–24	140	120
25–34	340	130
35–44	810	430
45–54	950	520
55–64	2,130	1,490
65–74	6,190	4,090
75–84	12,610	11,390
85+	12,530	21,160

Source: U.S. Centers for Disease Control, "Provisional numbers of deaths for the 10 leading causes of death by age, race and sex, United States, 1992," *Monthly Vital Statistics*, September 28, 1993.

In the United States, by the time they are 50, there are equal numbers of men and women. In the 1990 U.S. Census, there were only 67 males for every 100 females older than 65, and only 46 males for every 100 females older than 80. At age 95, American women outnumber men by four to one.

Worldwide population figures show slightly more men than women overall; in 1990, there were 1,014 males for every 1,000 females. The country with the lowest ratio of men to women is the Ukraine, where there are only 1,000 males for every 1,153 females. The country with the most men per women is the United Arab Emirates, where there are an extraordinary 1,000 males for every 493 females. The United States is right in the middle: 1,210 males for every 1,274 females.

The ratio of men to women may have important consequences for the stability of MARRIAGES. In 1995, Scott J. Smith professor of sociology at the State University of New York in Albany, published a report suggesting that the number of men available affects the divorce rate. In a six-year survey of 2,592 men and women (non-Hispanic white people in their 20s interviewed each year from 1979 to 1985), Smith found that divorce is most likely during the early years of marriage in cities or towns where the ratio of men to women is either very high or very low. At 162 men for every 100 women, the risk of divorce went up 13 percent; at 105 men for every 100 women, it rose 8 percent. Divorce was least likely when the ratio was somewhere in the middle, 129 men for every 100 women. The clear implication is that competition for mates upsets stable relationships and may lead to an excess number of divorces when there are either "too many" or "not enough" eligible men (or women) available. Theoretically, you might assume that when there are more men than "needed," the competition would be initiated by the males; when there are more women, by the females. Either way, the stability of marriages falls victim to an out-of-kilter sex ratio.

porphyrias   The porphyrias are inherited enzyme deficiencies that inhibit the body's ability to synthesize heme, the red pigment in blood cells that carries oxygen and iron throughout the body. Most porphyrias occur as often in men as in women; however, two—acute intermittent porphyria and porphyria cutanea tarda—are gender-related, the first more common in women, the second more common in men.

Acute intermittent porphyria, which occurs most frequently in Lapland, Scandinavia, and the United Kingdom, affects women more often than men. Its symptoms include muscle weakness, abdominal pain, gastrointestinal problems (nausea, vomiting, constipation, diarrhea), and, occasionally, seizures.

Porphyria cutanea tarda (PCT) is usually associated with the abuse of alcohol or drugs or the use of estrogens. Once more common among men, PCT is now growing in incidence among women, almost certainly because of the increasing use of estrogens in birth control pills and in postmenopausal hormone replacement therapy. PCT causes skin lesions or pigmentation changes on parts of the skin exposed to light.

pregnancy   There are three basic reasons why men cannot become pregnant. First, they do not produce eggs. Second, they do not have a uterus to house the growing fetus. Third, they do not have the hormones required to sustain a pregnancy.

Modern technology can easily address the first and third problems, by implanting a fertilized egg and injecting the required hormones. But can the fetus grow in a womb-less male body? Perhaps.

Each month, a fertile woman's ovary releases a mature egg that moves down the fallopian tube and into the uterus to meet the approaching sperm. Once in every 100 to 200 pregnancies, the egg is fertilized and implants in a place other than the uterus, a phenomenon known as an ectopic pregnancy. The overwhelming majority of ectopic pregnancies occur in the fallopian tubes; these pregnancies are surgically terminated to prevent a potentially fatal rupture of the tube. On very rare occasions, the egg released by the ovary slips out of the fallopian tube into the abdomen, where it is fertilized and implants in the abdominal wall.

Abdominal pregnancies are rare and potentially hazardous, but some have been brought to term. In theory, this kind of pregnancy could be created in the male body using the sac formed by the omentum, a fold of the peritoneum that hangs down in front of the intestines. If a fertilized egg inserted into the male abdomen through a small incision were to attach itself to the omentum, a placenta would develop and pregnancy would be under way.

In fact, scientists have already done this with at least one male baboon as part of a study on ovarian cancer in which the researcher wanted to know at what point cancerous ovaries could be removed without imperiling the pregnancy. No such human male pregnancy has ever been attempted, but in 1994, after the Arnold Schwartzenegger movie *Junior* was released, science writer Dick Teresi recalled for the *New York Times* an article he had coauthored eight years earlier dealing specifically with this possibility.

At the time, Teresi had volunteered to try male pregnancy, but he pulled back at the last minute. "I began to think about the risks involved," he wrote. "Advanced abdominal pregnancy kills 10 percent of the women who experience it and 70 percent of their babies. What would it do to a man? And his baby? Like someone waking up from an intoxicating daydream, I came to my senses."

PROTEIN RECOMMENDED DIETARY ALLOWANCES

Age	RDA
11–14 years	
males	45 gm
females	46 gm
15–18 years	
males	59 gm
females	44 gm
19–24 years	
males	58 gm
females	46 gm
25–50 years	
males	63 gm
females	50 gm
51+ years	
males	63 gm
females	50 gm
Pregnant	60
Nursing	65/62

Source: National Research Council, *Recommended Dietary Allowances*, 10th ed. (Washington, D.C.: Academy of Sciences, 1989).

GOOD SOURCES OF PROTEIN

**Food Portions That Provide 50 Percent or More
of the RDA for Adults**

Meat, fish, poultry	3–3.5 oz
Soybeans	1 cup
Other beans, peas	1.5 cup

**Food Portions That Provide 8–15 Percent of the
RDA for Adults**

Milk	8 oz
Hard cheese	1 oz
Egg	1
Nuts	1–1.5 oz
Peanut butter	2 tbsp

Source: George M. Briggs and Doris Howes Callaway, *Nutrition and Physical Fitness* (New York: Holt, Rinehart and Winston, 1964), p. 88.

---

protein   Because protein requirements for healthy adults are determined by body weight, the recommended dietary allowances (RDA) are higher for men than for women.

Based on a recommended 0.75 grams of protein a day for every kilogram (2.2 pounds) of body weight, the RDA for a healthy man older than 25, weighing 174 pounds, is approximately 60 grams a day. For a healthy woman older than 25, weighing 139 pounds, the recommendation is approximately 50 grams.

When she is pregnant or nursing, a woman's protein requirement will rise. Throughout the three trimesters of pregnancy, her requirement is 60 grams a day, 10 grams above the requirement for a healthy woman who is not pregnant. In the first six months of nursing, a breastfeeding mother needs 65 grams of protein a day; in the second six months, 62 grams.

puberty   Because the ovaries begin to secrete adult levels of sex hormones earlier than the testes do, girls have been winning the race to puberty ever since people started keeping records on such things.

During the Middle Ages, the Catholic Church set the permissible age for marriage at 12 years for girls, 14 years for boys, almost certainly because these were the times when the first signs of puberty appeared. Medieval medical observers reliably recorded menarche (the first menstrual period) as occurring between 12 and 15, and boys may well have been experiencing a first ejaculation at age 14, although during the 18th century, the male VOICE often remained soprano as late as age 18. Today, thanks in part to better nutrition and better medical care, both boys and girls reach puberty at an increasingly younger age, but girls still get there before boys.

For girls, the first visible sign of sexual development is the appearance of "breast buds," a small enlargement of the breast tissue between the ages of eight and 11. Menarche generally follows approximately two years later. In the United States today, the average age at menarche is 12 years and three months, but there is wide variation among healthy girls, and it is completely normal to experience a first period as early as ten or as late as 15 ½.

On average, boys now reach puberty at around age 13. The first sign of male sexual maturity is the thinning of the scrotum and growth of the testicles, usually between age ten and 12. The first ejaculation is likely to occur between the ages of 12 and 14, but as with menarche, variations are both possible and expected. By the time he is 14, a boy may be producing mature sperm, but he does not reach his maximum fertility until his late teens or even his early 20s. In both boys and girls, nipples begin to darken at around age 12 or 13; pubic hair first appears at age 11, and axillary hair (hair under the arms) a year or two later.

A girl who begins to mature sexually before age eight or a boy who starts before age ten is said to be going through "precocious puberty." True precocious puberty is an endocrine disorder caused by activity in the hypothalamus and pituitary glands that triggers the growth of the ovaries or testes, followed by the development of breasts and penis, formation of sperm, release of eggs, and the secretion of adult levels of sex hormones. A second form of precocious puberty may be caused by tumors that secrete hormones that trigger sexual development even as the ovaries and testes themselves remain immature. Girls are two to five times more likely than boys to experience true precocious puberty; 60 percent of the boys with premature puberty have an underlying illness such as a tumor of the hypothalamus, the brain, or the adrenal glands.

The opposite condition—delayed sexual maturity—is defined in boys as the absence of any testicle growth by age 13.5, or a lapse of more than five years' time between the beginning and end of genital growth. For girls, delayed sexual maturity means having no breast development by age 13 or experiencing a lapse of more than five years between the beginning of breast growth and the onset of the first menstrual period. Because sex hormones are also responsible for boys' and girls' growing taller, being abnormally short may also be a sign of sexual immaturity.

Q

quinine   Quinine is a drug used to prevent or treat malaria. It works equally
well in men and women, but it is also an abortifacient and a teratogen that poses
a special threat to women of childbearing age.

If a woman takes quinine while she is pregnant, the drug may trigger a
miscarriage or damage the fetus. The fetal problem most often associated with
quinine is deafness caused by injury to the auditory nerve. Vision changes and
deformities of the arms, legs, and internal organs have also been observed.

Other antimalarial drugs such as chloroquine (Aralen), hydroxychloroquine
(Atabrine), pyramethamine (Daraprim), and the combination of isulfadoxine
plus pyramethamine (Fansidar) may also be harmful to the fetus.

R

Raynaud's disease Raynaud's disease is a generally benign disorder that causes periodic spasms in the tiny BLOOD VESSELS (arterioles) at the tips of the fingers, toes, nose, and tongue. When the arterioles tighten, the flow of warm blood into the area decreases, the temperature in the tissues drops, and the skin may turn pale.

These spasms are most likely to occur when a person with Raynaud's is exposed to cold weather or touches very cold objects. They may also come after an emotional upset that sets off a stress reaction leading to the release of catecholamines, chemicals that make blood vessels expand or contract, diverting blood from the body's surface to the muscles and heart—one of a series of physical events collectively known as the "fight or flight" reaction.

Raynaud's disease is usually diagnosed for the first time in adolescence or early adulthood, between the ages of 15 and 45. As many as nine of every ten people with Raynaud's are women, and there are strong hints of a link between Raynaud's and migraine HEADACHES, which also strike many more women than men. The exact cause of Raynaud's remains a mystery, but it is common to find a family history of the condition.

reading Reading requires both intelligence and vision—the ability to see symbols (letters) and the capacity to translate them into words and concepts. Occasionally, a person with adequate vision and intelligence is unable to read because his or her brain processes visual images upside down or backwards, a condition called a reading disorder.

In 1994, a team of Yale University scientists looking for a physiological basis for reading disorders such as DYSLEXIA decided to use magnetic resonance imaging (MRI) to create pictures of blood flow in the brains of 19 men and 19

116

women volunteers while they were reading. When an area of the brain is active, it gets a continuous flow of fresh, oxygenated blood. Capturing this flow in MRI images would show which parts of the brain were being used.

To their surprise, the Yale scientists discovered that men and women appear to use different parts of their brains while reading. All the men in the study used a small portion at the front of the left side. Eight of the women also used this part of the brain, but ten of the women, a majority, also used part of the right side of the brain.

The female ability to use both sides of the brain while reading almost certainly arises from the fact that women have a relatively larger CORPUS CALLOSUM, the bundle of nerve fibers that connect the hemispheres. The increased number of connections may explain why women appear to recover more quickly from a stroke affecting one side of the brain. It may also turn out to explain why women are less likely to suffer from a reading disorder: When something goes awry on the left side, they simply switch to the right.

red blood cells   A healthy man normally has proportionately more red blood cells than a healthy woman—4.5–6.2 million red blood cells per cubic microliter of blood for men compared with 4–5.5 million for women.

The number of red blood cells in the body is based on different figures for men and women. A man has about 30 ml of cells for each kilogram (kg = 2.2 pounds) of weight, so a 70 kg (150-pound) man has about 2,100 ml of red blood cells in his body. A woman's has about 27 ml/kg; a 50 kg (110-pound) woman has 1,890 ml of red blood cells.

Because they have more red blood cells, men also have higher values of hemoglobin, the pigment in red blood cells that carries oxygen throughout the body. They also have higher levels of IRON, which is a constituent of hemoglobin.

reproductive hazards   A reproductive hazard is anything that interferes with an individual's ability to produce healthy offspring.

For women, a reproductive hazard is most commonly defined as anything that harms a developing fetus. For example, a pregnant woman's SMOKING can inhibit fetal heartbeat and respiration. A maternal diet lacking adequate calories or sufficient quantities of nutrients such as folic acid, one of the VITAMIN B COMPLEX, and/or exposure to medications such as QUININE, or to chemicals or radiation may cause birth defects.

For men, a reproductive hazard is something that reduces sperm production or damages sperm so that either they cannot fertilize an egg or they transmit a defect to the offspring. Because sperm are small and hard to track, it has taken much longer to identify male reproductive hazards. Sixteen years ago, American Cyanamid made headlines when it banned women of childbearing age from jobs that would expose them (and any possible fetus) to lead. What roiled the waters wasn't the company's seeking to protect women, but its failure to protect men.

Lead is a well-known hazard to male reproduction. At the University of Maryland, toxicologist Ellen Silbergeld has shown that offspring of male rats exposed to levels of lead equal to what's in the air of inner-city neighborhoods often have "substantial" brain damage. In February 1994, researchers at the University of California–Los Angeles School of Medicine released a report showing that high exposure to lead may reduce the level of testosterone circulating in the male body, altering sperm production *and* the power of sperm to

---

SOME KNOWN AND SUSPECTED OCCUPATIONAL HAZARDS TO MALE REPRODUCTIVE HEALTH

Chemical/ condition	Who's at risk	Observed or suspected effect of paternal exposure[*]
Glycol ethers	Workers in paint and semiconductors	Lowered sperm count
Heat	Bakers, foundry workers	Lowered sperm count
Hydrocarbons (solvents, metals, oils, and paints)	Garage mechanics, auto body workers, paint workers	Increased incidence of childhood kidney cancer in offspring
Lead	Paint and battery workers	Increased risk of miscarriage in partners; reduced levels of testosterone; increased risk of brain damage in offspring (animals)
Metal fumes	Welders	Increase in abnormal sperm
Pesticides	Farm workers, workers in pesticide plants	Lowered sperm count; increased risk of liver disorder in offspring
Radiation	Workers in nuclear plants, radar operators	Increased incidence of leukemia in offspring
Toxic smoke	Firefighters	Increased incidence of heart defects among offspring
Vinyl chloride	Rubber and tire workers	Increased incidence of miscarriage among partners

[*]Unless otherwise noted, effect is observed or suspected in human beings.

Source: Carol Ann Rinzler, *The Safe Pregnancy Book* (New York: New American Library, 1984), pp. 116–122.

fertilize eggs. Partners of men exposed to lead are more susceptible to MISCAR-
RIAGE, often a sign of an embryo/fetus with serious genetic damage.

Other potential hazards for men at work include pesticides, industrial solvents, high heat, and radiation. All reduce sperm counts; some may affect genetic
material. Michael Silverstein, director of policy for the Occupational Safety and
Health Administration (OSHA) in Washington, says the agency is working to
reduce exposure to a number of these chemicals. At the same time, occupational
physicians at the University of Southern California have created a study to
follow children of workers exposed to solvents on the job. But many suspected
reproductive hazards in the workplace remain unregulated.

reproductive organs   Although they look entirely different, the male and
female reproductive organs arise from the same embryonic tissue.

For example, the ovaries and testes both develop from a potential ovary. In
a female fetus, the potential ovary becomes a true ovary. In a male fetus, a gene
or group of genes on the Y chromosome, known as testis determining factor
(TDF), begins to exert its effects near the end of the second month of pregnancy,
converting the potential ovary into a testis. The same tissue has now become
two different types of organs, one male, one female.

The urogenital systems arise from either the Wolffian or the Müllerian ducts,
two channels that lie side by side down the length of the embryonic body. In a
male fetus, once TDF becomes active, the Müllerian duct disappears under the
influence of hormones secreted by the embryonic testes, leaving the Wolffian
duct, which gives rise to the epidymides (a storage depot next to the testes in
which sperm mature), the vas deferens (a tube that carries sperm from the testes
to the prostate), and the seminal vesicles (which manufacture part of the seminal
fluid). In the female, the Wolffian duct disappears, leaving the Müllerian duct
to evolve into the fallopian tubes, the uterus, and the upper part of the vagina.

As late as the 12th week of pregnancy, the only sign of external genitalia in
either a male or a female fetus is a bump in the genital area made up of several
distinct components that, under the influence of testosterone or estrogen, will
differentiate into the male or female urogenital system. The urogenital sinus will
become the prostate and the upper part of the urethra in the male or the urethra
and lower part of the vagina in the female. The genital tubercle will become the
head of the penis or the clitoris in the female. The urogenital swellings will
become the scrotum or the large, outer lips of the vagina. Finally, the urethral
folds will become the small vaginal lips or will join together to create the male
urethra and the shaft of the penis.

COMPARABLE STRUCTURES IN THE MALE/FEMALE
REPRODUCTIVE SYSTEMS

Male	Female
Testes	Ovaries
Scrotum	Labia majora (large, outer lips of the vagina)
Underside of penis	Labia minora (small, inner lips of the vagina)
Glans (head) of the penis	Glans (tip) of the clitoris
Corpus cavernosum (erectile tissue of the penis)	Shaft (erectile tissue of the clitoris)
Cowper's glands (mucus glands on either side of the urethra)	Bartholin's glands (mucus glands on either side of the vagina)

Source: The Boston Women's Collective, *The New Our Bodies, Ourselves* (New York: Simon & Schuster, 1992); Simon LeVay, *The Sexual Brain* (Cambridge, MA: MIT Press, 1994); *The Visual Dictionary of the Human Body* (New York: Dorling, Kindersley, 1991).

Given this history, it is not surprising to find that many components of the male and female reproductive systems have analogous functions. Both ovaries and testes feed GERM CELLS through tubes into, respectively, the uterus and the top of the penis. The cells (egg and sperm) then move either down into the uterus or out through the penis, to meet each other.

The tip of the penis and the tip of the clitoris are composed of similarly sensitive erectile tissue; the body of the penis and the sides of the vagina are similarly expandable tissue. In both sexes, special mucus glands (Cowper's for men; Bartholin's for women) lubricate the reproductive organs.

rheumatic heart disease   Although there is no gender difference in susceptibility to rheumatic heart disease, more men than women die of the disease, suggesting (but not proving) that the male heart may be damaged more severely by the illness.

In 1990, the American Heart Association reported nearly twice as many rheumatic heart deaths among men as among women—4,188 male deaths versus 1,830 female deaths.

S

scoliosis   Scoliosis—from the Greek word for "a crookedness"—is a side-ways curvature of the spine. It may be caused by habitual bad posture, by a disease of the spine, by a weakness or spasm of the muscles of the back, or simply by one leg's being shorter than the other.

Depending on the reason for the scoliosis, there may be more than one curve. In addition, the "s" formed by the curving spine may be "fixed" (unmoving) if the muscle and bone are deformed or may be "mobile" (movable) if the muscles alone are at fault.

In childhood, scoliosis is more common among boys, but scoliosis due to an asymmetrical development of the muscle and nerves is approximately four to five times more common in girls. This kind of scoliosis usually produces no symptoms early in life. Later on, however, the strong curvature may cause back pain or may position the body so as to constrict the lungs, making it more difficult to breathe.

sebaceous glands   The sebaceous glands, located just under the top layer of skin cells, secrete a slick, oily substance called sebum. Sebum is beneficial because it smoothes and lubricates the skin, but it may also block pores, creating an environment that supports the growth of bacteria associated with ACNE.

Because the activity of the sebaceous glands is regulated by the male sex hormones, specifically testosterone, the amount of sebum on the skin is a good guide to how much testosterone the body is producing.

At PUBERTY, when testosterone levels rise, the sebaceous glands spring to life. Sebum production reaches a peak in late adolescence, then remains rela-tively stable until a woman approaches menopause or a man moves into his 70s. At menopause, when hormone levels decline, sebum production declines, too.

In old age, a woman may be producing less than half as much sebum as she did during her reproductive years.

But a man's secretion of testosterone and his sebum production hold steady until he is well into his late 70s, at which time he may be producing twice as much sebum as a woman his own age. This difference in sebum production among the elderly is one reason why older women are more likely than older men to complain about dry skin or to develop facial WRINKLES.

selenium   Selenium is a trace element whose necessity in the human diet was not established until 1979. Its precise function in the body remains obscure, but it is believed to work in concert with vitamin E, as an antioxidant nutrient. The recommended dietary allowance (RDA) for selenium is based on body weight—0.87 micrograms of selenium for each kilogram (2.2 pounds) of body weight. This works out to approximately 70 micrograms a day for adult men and 55 micrograms a day for adult women. Good sources of selenium include seafood, organ meats (kidneys and liver), and to a lesser extent, other meats.

sex chromosomes   Human beings normally have 46 chromosomes—22 pairs of autosomes (chromosomes other than the sex chromosomes) and two sex chromosomes, the X chromosome and the Y chromosome. An individual with two X chromosomes is female; an individual with one X chromosome and one Y chromosome is male.

The X chromosome carries genes for a number of BIRTH DEFECTS and inherited X-LINKED TRAITS such as COLOR BLINDNESS and HEMOPHILIA. X-linked traits (sometimes called "sex-linked traits") commonly affect men; women are generally carriers.

The Y chromosome, shaped like a rod with a short arm branching off the main trunk, is distinguished by its ability to turn the embryo from a female default mode to male, via "testis determining factor" (TDF), one or more genes located on the short arm of the Y chromosome. TDF converts what would have been an ovary into a testis, which then produces testosterone that influences the muscles and genitals. Sperm carrying the Y chromosome appear to swim faster and to penetrate the egg more easily than sperm carrying an X chromosome, thus accounting for the higher male CONCEPTION AND BIRTH RATES.

Occasionally, a person is born carrying either more or fewer than 46 chromosomes, a condition called aneuploidy. Aneuploidy occurs when a pair of chromosomes fails to separate correctly as egg or sperm are being formed. DOWN'S SYNDROME is an example of a defect due to the presence of an extra chromosome. Other chromosomal aneuplodies involve the sex chromosomes.

These include Klinefelter's syndrome (a male born with an extra X chromosome, usually infertile, with a higher-than-normal risk of breast cancer); XYY (a male with an extra Y chromosome sometimes associated with a more aggressive personality); Turner's syndrome (a female who has only one X chromosome, does not mature sexually, and requires estrogen supplements); and XXX syndrome (a female with an extra X chromosome). Most fetuses with aneuploidy do not survive to term.

sex hormones   Sex hormones are naturally occurring steroid compounds that control the development of secondary sex characteristics such as facial and body HAIR and influence the activity of various body organs. Both men and women secrete both male and female hormones. It is the balance between the two, not the total absence of one or the other, that makes us look, and to some extent behave, like males or females.

The male sex hormones are known collectively as androgens. The primary androgen is testosterone. Most testosterone is created by testicular conversion of another steroid compound, cholesterol. But smaller amounts of testosterone are produced in both men and women by converting cholesterol to testosterone in the adrenal glands.

There are two female sex hormones, estrogen and progesterone. Most of the estrogen in the body is produced by converting cholesterol to estrogen in the ovaries. Smaller amounts are manufactured by the conversion of cholesterol in body fat or by converting testosterone to estrogen at various sites throughout the body, including the brain. The three most potent and plentiful estrogens are estradiol, the principle estrogen secreted by the ovaries; estrone, which is made primarily in body fat; and estriol, created when the body metabolizes estradiol and estrone. Estriol is the most plentiful estrogen in urine.

The second female hormone, progesterone, is secreted by the corpus luteum, a glandular area of the ovary. Progesterone is vital to the development of the placenta. It also relaxes the smooth muscle of the pregnant uterus and stimulates the development of milk-producing glands for nursing. Rising levels of progesterone seem to disrupt a pregnant woman's sleep patterns, causing the common INSOMNIA of pregnancy. On the other hand, when estrogen secretion declines at menopause, women may experience sleep disturbances once again.

The male and female sex hormones produce specific effects at every stage of life. While the fetus is still in the womb, testis determining factor (TDF), a gene on the Y chromosome, turns potential ovaries into testes that secrete testosterone, which triggers the development of male reproductive organs, a longer, heavier male body, and a male brain with a relatively larger right hemisphere.

Testosterone produced by the male FETUS also affects its mother; women carrying males are more prone to a number of problems during pregnancy, including swollen hands and face.

From birth to adolescence, the sex hormones remain relatively quiescent. They become active once again at PUBERTY, nudging the physical development of male and female bodies along different paths. Testosterone encourages the growth of long, heavy bones, wide SHOULDERS, narrow HIPS, and bulkier, energy-hungry MUSCLE tissue, while estrogen stimulates the accumulation of fatty tissue—energy reserves in the BREASTS, hips, and buttocks.

Because ovaries mature and become active earlier than testes, sex hormones rise to adult levels earlier in the female body, and girls generally enter puberty at an earlier age than boys. Later in life, a woman's estrogen levels drop precipitously while older men continue to produce relatively large amounts of sex hormones.

The effects of the postmenopausal decline in estrogen production are clear-cut and precise. Because she no longer ovulates, a woman is no longer fertile [see FERTILITY, INFERTILITY]. Without estrogen to protect bone density, she is at higher risk of OSTEOPOROSIS, her SKIN is drier, thinner, and more likely to wrinkle, and her HAIR thins.

Men do not experience this sudden change. While there is a progressive decline in testosterone levels as a man grows older—and it seems reasonable to blame this for a corresponding slow decline in libido—as well as in muscle mass and physical strength, even in old age the testes may continue to secrete sufficient testosterone to produce enough viable sperm to keep a man fertile.

sexual arousal   Sexual arousal is a series of physical events that facilitate sexual intercourse. Because men's and women's REPRODUCTIVE ORGANS are biologically similar, sexual arousal follows similar paths in male and female bodies. For both, there is a suddenly increased flow of blood to vessels in the pelvic/genital area. In men, this allows the spongy tissue inside the penis to expand into an erection. In women, it firms the clitoris, as the walls of the vagina begin to secrete lubricating fluid.

At the same time, both men and women experience a generalized muscle tension throughout the body. Blood pressure rises. The heart beats faster. Breathing quickens. The skin may flush and perspire. Muscle tissue around the nipples tightens and the nipples stand erect. There are the beginnings of contractions in the pelvic area, accompanied by an involuntary but pleasurable thrusting of the pelvis.

Each step in sexual arousal—erection, lubrication, perspiration, pelvic contractions—is controlled by the autonomic nervous system, the body's automatic pilot responsible for such basic functions as heartbeat, respiration, metabolism, blood flow and so forth. Because the autonomic nervous system responds immediately to emotional stimuli such as pleasure, fear, and anger, any unpleasant conditions—a cold room, a psychological distraction, fatigue—can bring sexual arousal to a dead halt.

In most cases, sexual arousal proceeds in a straight line to sexual completion: ORGASM. Cultural wisdom and a variety of studies suggest that men are more easily aroused by direct sexual contact or exposure to sexually explicit material, but this is still very much open to question. It may simply be that the universal sign of male arousal, an erect penis, is more visible.

For both men and women, the ability to become sexually aroused depends greatly on psychological as well as physical triggers. Touch is arousing, but so

SOME MEDICATIONS THAT AFFECT
LIBIDO AND SEXUAL AROUSAL

Medication	Who is affected	Observed effect
Androgens (male hormones)	Men and women	Increased libido
Antialcohol drugs	Men and possibly women	Decreased libido
Antiangina (digitalis)	Men	Impotence
Antianxiety drugs	Men and women	Contradictory effects: increased libido due to feeling of well-being; but also decreased libido and possibility of male impotence
Antidepressants	Men and women	Impaired sexual arousal
Antihistamines	Men and possibly women	Decreased libido; impotence
Betablockers (blood pressure medicine)	Men and possibly women	Decreased libido; impotence
Diuretics	Men	Impotence
Estrogens and medroxyprogesterone (female hormones)	Men	Decreased libido
Sedatives and tranquilizers	Men and possibly women	Decreased libido

Source: James W. Long and James J. Rybacki, *The Essential Guide to Prescription Drugs* (New York: HarperCollins, 1994).

is the sight of a welcome sexual partner. For women, the feel of a baby's feeding from the breast may be arousing. It is often believed that small touches of intimacy are more important for women than for men, but in fact, men, too, may find it hard to become aroused or to reach a climax without a sense of intimate engagement.

Sometimes sexual arousal is inhibited by a medical condition or by the medication used to treat it. For men, DIABETES, an inflammation of the pelvic or genital area, a neurological disorder such as MULTIPLE SCLEROSIS, prostate disease, or the removal of the prostate gland makes it difficult to achieve or sustain an erection. For women, a localized disease such as endometriosis or cystitis can make intercourse painful. For both sexes, a muscular or neurological disorder such as MUSCULAR DYSTROPHY or multiple sclerosis may inhibit arousal.

shoulders   Broad shoulders are a male secondary sex characteristic. Testosterone makes a man's shoulder bones broader and his muscles bulkier, giving him upper body PHYSICAL STRENGTH estimated to be as much as three times greater than a woman's. Broader shoulders give a man the edge when it comes to throwing a ball straight and fast [see ARM].

skeleton   There are 265 BONES in the human skeleton (from the Greek word for "dried up"). As a rule, all male bones are larger than the corresponding female bones and show more "markings"—spots where the heavier male MUSCLES rub against the bone.

A number of bones and bone groupings are reliable guides to the gender of a naked skeleton. For example, the male SKULL is larger, and the chin is square rather than rounded or pointed like the female chin. The male PELVIS is narrower and deeper in relation to the body; the female pelvis is broad and shallow. The male SHOULDERS are broader; and the long bones of the ARMS and LEGS are longer and heavier.

skin   The skin is an organ, the largest in the body. An average man's skin stretches to cover an area approximately 20 feet square and weighs about ten pounds. An average woman's skin covers about 17.5 square feet and weighs slightly less than a man's. Male skin is microscopically thicker than female skin. Because thinner skin is damaged more easily by sunlight, physical injury, and mechanical stress, and because an older woman's SEBACEOUS GLANDS produce less lubricating sebum, a woman's face WRINKLES earlier than a man's.

skin tags   A skin tag is a soft wart frequently found on the shoulders of elderly women, but rarely on the shoulders of elderly men. Skin tags are unsightly but nonthreatening, and they are easily removed. Just about the only interesting fact anyone has ever uncovered regarding skin tags comes from a 1976 study published in *The New England Journal of Medicine* suggesting that skin tags on a man's body may be an early warning sign of diabetes. Examining 500 patients (480 men, 20 women) admitted to a veterans' hospital in Texas, the researchers found that 34 of the 47 men with skin tags had diabetes.

skull   It is relatively easy to tell a male skull from a female skull. It's bigger overall, and so are its component parts—the sinus cavities, the protective bone hollows surrounding the eyes, the lower JAW, the palate, the TEETH, and the chin.

In addition, the muscle markings on a male skull are generally deeper and more pronounced, particularly where the larger male facial muscles continually rub against the prominence of the forehead, at the arches where the facial bones are joined, at the ridge at the back of the neck, and in the spots where the muscles that open and close the lower jaw attach to the skull.

sleep   A healthy adult sleeps approximately 7 ½ to 8 ½ hours a night. Women generally sleep slightly longer than men; a 1989 study from the National Bureau of Economic Research puts the difference at about 2 percent of sleep time or approximately 9 ½ minutes.

Women complain more about INSOMNIA. They are also more likely to have trouble getting to sleep, but once they drift off, they sleep more quietly, move less often, stay asleep better, and have longer periods of rapid eye movement (REM) sleep—the sleep during which dreaming occurs. Men are more susceptible to sleep disorders such as BED-WETTING, NIGHTMARES, SLEEP APNEA, and SLEEPWALKING. In old age, they are less likely than women to sleep through the night, and they have shorter periods of deep, dreamless sleep, the sleep that refreshes.

Despite the disparities in their sleep behavior, men and women do like to sleep together, but they have different reasons for enjoying a shared bed. In 1994, researchers Francesca Pankhurst and James Horne of Longborough University in Leicestershire, England monitored sleep in 46 pairs of bed partners, 23 to 67 years old, for eight nights. Eighty-four percent slept together in a double bed; 16 percent, in a king-sized bed. The researchers compared their sleeping behavior with that of 39 people of the same age and sex who habitually slept alone. What they found was that people who share a bed do not sleep as soundly as people who sleep alone.

The Longborough study showed that when one bed partner moves, the other does, too, usually within 30 seconds. Because sleeping men move around more frequently than sleeping women, women are disturbed more often by their partners. Older partners reacted less to their mates' movements; perhaps people become accustomed to a particular partner's sleep patterns.

At the end of the study, it was clear that when couples slept alone and apart from each other, perhaps because a partner was away for the night, both slept longer and more peacefully. But they didn't think they did. In fact, both the men and the women adamantly insisted they slept better with their partners next to them. The women said it was because they felt more secure when sleeping with their partner. The men said it was because they had gotten used to sharing a bed.

sleep apnea   Sleep apnea is a disorder that causes the victim to stop breathing for several seconds at a time, up to hundreds of times a night. According to Steve K. Watson of the New Haven, Connecticut Sleep Disorders Clinic, these pauses in breathing lower the level of oxygen in the blood, intermittently depriving the brain of oxygen and interfering with brain functioning.

Sleep apnea is 12 to 15 times more common among men. It is estimated that as many as one in every 20 American men may have trouble with attention, concentration, or memory—enough to lower their IQ approximately 10 points—because of it. Why this should be so is still unknown, but some blame the heavier male NECK, twisting and blocking the airway in sleep. Sleep apnea is particularly common among obese men, who also snore more often. Although obese women may also experience this problem, there is at least the hint of a hormone-based sex difference, because sleep apnea is rarely seen in pre-menopausal women.

Data from a 1990 233-patient apnea study at Montefiore Medical Center in New York showed that while men are more likely than women to have sleep apnea, women patients are at particularly high risk of death. Montefiore researcher Bernard Burack concludes that sleep apnea can double a person's risk of dying from heart disease.

sleepwalking   When things go bump in the night, the person most likely to end up with a bruised shin from sleepwalking into the furniture is a man.

About 15 percent of all children between the ages of five and 12 sleepwalk at least once. Up to 6 percent of all children sleepwalk persistently; most of these young sleepwalkers are boys. The difference between boys and girls is real, says Richard Ferber, director of the Center for Pediatric Sleep Disorders at the Children's Hospital in Boston. When sleep scientists ask parents simply whether their children sleepwalk, they get the same numbers for boys and girls. But if there is a second, more direct question, such as who sleepwalks more often, the boys always come out ahead.

Sleep researchers regard sleepwalking among children as a sign of immaturity, saying that boys sleepwalk more often than girls because boys mature later. A gender difference persists into adulthood, when slightly more men than women are likely to visit sleep clinics complaining of sleepwalking, says Stephen A. Burton, assistant director at the Sleep Disorder and Research Center at Rush Presbyterian–St. Luke's Hospital Center in Chicago.

smell, sense of   Like the sense of HEARING, the sense of smell waxes and wanes in a circadian rhythm controlled by the secretion of adrenal hormones. On a normal sleep/wake cycle, both senses peak at around 2 A.M. to 3 A.M., but at every point in the cycle, a woman's sense of smell will be sharper than a man's, says Robert Henkin, director of the Taste and Smell Clinic at the Center for Molecular Nutrition and Sensory Disorders in Washington, D.C.

Young or old, women tend to do better on tests measuring sensitivity to odors. Because a woman's acuity parallels her monthly production of hormones, reaching a peak at ovulation and then declining through the rest of the cycle, there is a strong circumstantial link to female hormones—a link evident even before the onset of puberty. As Diane Ackermann points out in *The Natural History of the Senses*, even girls who have not yet reached puberty do better than boys. "Women in general just have a stronger sense of smell," Ackermann writes. "Perhaps it is a vestigial bonus from the dawn of our evolution when we needed it in courtship, mating or mothering."

In young people, anosmia—the loss of the sense of smell—is most often linked to a viral infection. In the elderly, anosmia more commonly follows a head injury.

smokers   In the United States, smoking has always been predominantly a male habit. Even now, male smokers outnumber females 25.4 million to 23 million; these figures represent 28 percent of all American men versus 24 percent of the women.

The trend is down for both men and women. From 1965 to 1991, the percentage of men who smoke dropped 15 points, from 43 percent to 28 percent. In the same period, the percentage of women smokers dropped from 33 percent to 24 percent. In all, 44 million Americans, nearly half of all the living adults in this country who had ever smoked, had quit. By 1994, the Federal Centers for Disease Control reported another 1 percent drop among women smokers, to 23 percent.

However, as smoking declines among women overall, it is rising among young women. In 1990, 25.6 of American women aged 18 to 44 were smokers; in 1991, that rose to 26.9 percent. Most of the increase is due to an increase in smoking among young white women using cigarettes as a diet aid. From 1987 to 1992, the percentage of black women aged 18 to 24 who smoke dropped from 21.8 percent to 5.9 percent. Among white women in this age group it remained at 27 percent.

smoking, effects of   Some of the effects of smoking appear to be gender-related. For example, men who smoke are 22 times more likely than male nonsmokers to die from lung cancer; the risk for female smokers is 12 times higher than for women who do not smoke.

While smoking appears to decrease a person's ability to perceive pain, a 1994 study of 251 women aged 15 through 44 suggests that women who smoke are more likely to have painful menstrual periods, perhaps because smoking narrows blood vessels. Smoking reduces a woman's blood level of estrogen, perhaps because chemicals in tobacco smoke damage hormone-producing cells in the ovaries or cause the liver to inactivate estrogens more quickly. As a result, women who smoke do have a lower risk of estrogen-stimulated uterine cancers, but they may also reach menopause earlier, so their risk of osteoporosis rises. According to a survey of 41 pairs of female twins conducted at the University of Melbourne (Australia), when she reaches menopause, a woman who has smoked one pack of cigarettes a day throughout her adult life may expect her bones to be 5 percent to 10 percent less dense than if she had never smoked.

When a pregnant woman smokes, her FETUS does, too. Sonograms have shown that when the woman inhales, her baby's heart skips a beat. Newborns delivered by mothers who smoked during pregnancy are often low birth weight infants, and there is some evidence that even apparently healthy babies born to women who smoked during pregnancy have abnormally narrowed airways that may increase the infants' own risk of asthma and other respiratory problems. A pregnant woman's smoking may also produce subtle HEARING defects in the fetus [see REPRODUCTIVE HAZARDS].

Men do not escape unscathed. Male smokers are more likely than nonsmokers to produce abnormal sperm, and smoking may interfere with male sexual performance. In 1991, researchers at Boston University School of Medicine and University Hospital proposed a link between impotence and penile artery disease among young smokers who had no history of earlier blood vessel disease. Examining the medical histories and penile X-rays of 195 young (average age, 35) men suffering from impotence, and taking other risk factors into account, the scientists concluded that male smokers were more likely than nonsmokers to suffer from smoking-related damage to the penile arteries, similar to the coronary artery damage found in older smokers. Smoking one pack of cigarettes a day for five years led to a 15 percent increase in the risk of penile artery blockage leading to impotence. The risk for men who smoked a pack a day for 20 years was 72 percent higher than for nonsmokers. The penis, the researchers wrote, is an organ that depends on blood flowing in and out freely. Cigarettes slow the flow of blood, making it difficult to produce an effective erection.

snoring   The noise of snoring is caused by movements of the soft palate and other structures at the back of the mouth that vibrate when air is breathed in. Snoring is more common among people who are overweight or who smoke or who regularly consume alcoholic beverages. Men snore more often and more loudly than women.

The first large epidemiological survey on snoring was conducted in 1980 among 2,858 men and 2,855 women in San Marino, the world's first independent republic. It showed that about 24 percent of the men and 14 percent of the women in San Marino were habitual snorers. In a 1985 study in Finland, 9 percent of adult men and 3.6 percent of adult women reported that they "always" or "almost always" snore. A 1990 survey of respiratory disease among 1,222 Hispanic-American adults showed 27.8 percent of the men and 15.3 percent of the women to be regular, loud snorers.

Since then, this ratio has held through nearly 40 studies on sleep behavior ranging from "snoring always or almost always," snoring "often or always," and just plain "snoring." No matter how you describe it, regardless of race or ethnicity, more men are likely to snore more frequently and usually more noisily than women.

spatial reasoning   Men almost always score higher than women on tests designed to measure spatial reasoning. Men are better able to visualize what an object will look like if it is rotated in space—a skill useful in mathematics, engineering, and architecture, professions still dominated by men. This male superiority is so universal that it even crosses species lines. For example, male laboratory rats almost always perform better than female rats at running mazes.

People have tried to explain this difference in terms of intelligence or cultural conditioning or even a bias in the test or in the person running it, but recent brain studies suggest a purely physical explanation. In the male brain, the right hemisphere, which controls visual and spatial skills, is noticeably larger than it is in women. Just as women may derive an advantage in LANGUAGE AND SPEECH because they have more nerve cells connecting the two sides of the brain [see CORPUS CALLOSUM], the larger right hemisphere may give men an edge when it comes to spatial reasoning.

stillbirths   More males are stillborn, regardless of whether the pregnancy goes to term or delivery is premature. One large survey in the United States has put the ratio at 134 male full-term stillbirths to every 100 females.

Some studies imply that the male to female ratio is higher during a first pregnancy or among fetuses conceived by couples of different races, or among fetuses carried by a woman with blood type AB or who is older than 50. Regardless of gender, stillbirth is more common among blood type O fetuses, and among fetuses conceived by men who have been exposed to radiation—for example, men who survived the Hiroshima and Nagasaki bombs.

GENDER RATIO OF STILLBIRTHS		
Time of Delivery	**First Baby** **Boys:Girls**	**Later Baby** **Boys:Girls**
Premature birth	84:100	123:100
Full-term	128:100	109:100

Source: Richard L. Naeye and Nebiat Tafari, *Risk Factors in Pregnancy and Diseases of the Fetus and Newborn* (Baltimore: Williams & Wilkins, 1983), p. 318.

stomach cancer   In 1995, the American Cancer Society estimated 22,800 new cases of stomach cancer (14,000 among men, 8,800 among women) and 14,700 deaths (8,800 among men, 5,900 among women). The most likely candidate for stomach cancer is a man older than 50.

Over the last 50 years, there has been a steep decline in the incidence and the number of deaths from stomach cancer for both sexes, but the risk is still greater for men. In the early 1930s, there were approximately 38 deaths from stomach cancer for every 100,000 American men and 28 for every 100,000 American women. By 1989–1991, this had fallen to seven deaths per 100,000 men and three deaths per 100,000 women. Most experts attribute this decline to the widespread use of preservatives and methods of food storage that reduce spoilage, particularly spoilage from molds that produce carcinogenic aflatoxins.

stroke   According to the American Heart Association, the overall incidence of stroke is about 19 percent higher among men than among women; before age 65, the difference is even greater. After age 74, however, more women suffer stroke—because there are more women left alive [see LIFE EXPECTANCY].

ESTIMATED DEATHS FROM STROKE, 1992		
Age	Males	Females
Less than 1 yr.	20	—
1–14	60	80
15–24	80	40
25–34	370	380
35–44	1,640	1,240
45–54	2,350	2,280
55–64	5,100	4,640
65–74	12,650	12,170
75–84	21,170	29,030
85+	13,340	37,980

Source: U.S. Centers for Disease Control, "Provisional numbers of deaths for the 10 leading causes of death by age, race and sex, United States, 1992," *Monthly Vital Statistics*, September 28, 1993.

Women who suffer a stroke, particularly one affecting the left side of the brain where LANGUAGE AND SPEECH skills are located, are likely to regain functions more quickly and more completely. The female advantage may be due to a difference in the anatomy of the BRAIN: The female brain has a larger CORPUS CALLOSUM, the bundle of nerve cells that connects the hemispheres. As a result, women may be able to switch functions more easily from one side of the brain to the other, allowing the healthy hemisphere to take over when needed.

stuttering   No one inherits a stutter, but the tendency to focus stress-related tension at a TARGET AREA in the muscles of the larynx can be passed along from parent to child, most often from father to son. According to Martin Schwartz, executive director of the National Center for Stuttering, four times as many boys as girls experience stress-related vocal cord spasms that can lead to stuttering.

Sometimes the father doesn't know he's a potential stutterer. He may have only a weak tendency to clench his laryngeal muscles, never reaching the level of stress that triggers the lock that leads to the stutter. But his son's tendency is stronger. At some point, early in life, perhaps between the ages of two and seven, the child experiences stress great enough to reach his "locking threshold." At that moment, he cannot force air past his vocal cords. He cannot speak. He begins to struggle to release the lock; the struggle becomes habit; the habit is stuttering.

Forcing a LEFT-HANDED child to write with his right hand may bring him to the locking threshold, Dr. Schwartz explains, because it interferes with natural, instinctive brain–hand coordination. Ordinarily, the left side of the human brain controls movement on the right side of the body, while the right side of the brain controls movement on the left side of the body. A right-handed person uses the left side of his or her brain for speaking *and* writing. A left-handed person also uses the left side of the brain for speaking, but the right side of the brain for writing.

Left-handers do this instinctively, without thinking. Compelling a change to the right hand means forcing a left-hander to stop and think every time he or she picks up a pencil. Although some people make the switch without a hitch, others end up translating the stress into muscle-crunching tension that produces pain in the hinge of the jaw, lower back pain—or, if the target area is the vocal cords, spasms that turn a normal left-hander into a right-handed stutterer.

suicide   Suicide is the ninth leading cause of death in the United States. According to the Federal Centers for Disease Control, males are more likely both to attempt suicide and to succeed in the effort. In 1992, for example, there were an estimated 24,250 male versus 5,500 female suicides, a ratio of about five to one.

But the numbers of men and women who attempt suicide are more nearly equal. Three of every four men who attempt suicide succeed; among women, only one in four succeeds. Using these numbers as a guide, one may postulate 32,300 male versus 22,000 female attempted suicides in 1992. Men still outnumber women, but only by three to two.

San Diego, California sociologist David E. Phillips has found that white, middle-aged married men are more likely to commit suicide at the ages of 40 or 65 than at any other times in their lives, perhaps because these birthdays have become symbolic of aging. But suicide is not the prerogative solely of adults.

REPORTED DEATHS FROM SUICIDE, 1991		
Age	**Male**	**Female**
All ages	24,769	*
1–14 (yrs.)	208	*
15–34	9,434	1,831
35–54	7,454	2,296
55–74	4,983	*
75+	*	*

*Suicide is not among the ten leading causes of death in this group.

Source: National Center for Health Statistics, *Vital Statistics of the United States, 1991* (Washington, D.C.: Public Health Service, 1994).

ESTIMATED DEATHS FROM SUICIDE, 1992

Age	Male	Female
Less than 1 yr.	—	—
1–14	220	90
15–24	3,970	690
25–34	4,980	1,050
35–44	4,650	1,090
45–54	2,970	1,000
55–64	2,390	650
65–74	2,120	500
75–84	2,430	350
85+	520	80

Source: U.S. Centers for Disease Control, "Provisional numbers of deaths for the 10 leading causes of death by age, race and sex, United States, 1992," *Monthly Vital Statistics*, September 28, 1993.

Among adolescents, it is second only to accidents as a cause of death, with an estimated 13.8 suicides per 100,000 adolescents. These are minimum figures, because with suicide, intention must be proved—that is, it must be shown that the death did not result from an accidental gunshot or car crash. In other words, it is possible that many "accidental" deaths are really suicides. Once again, the victims are more likely to be male. For young adults aged 15 to 19, males are 400 percent more likely to commit suicide; white males are most at risk; and girls are more likely than boys to attempt suicide and fail.

While the incidence of suicide by gunshot varies from city to city and from state to state, depending on how hard it is to get a firearm, guns are increasingly the instrument of choice. In 1978, 58 percent of all male suicides used a firearm; in 1980, it was 63 percent, with guns accounting for 16,285 self-inflicted deaths.

SUICIDES INVOLVING GUNS

Age	Male	Female
5–14 yr.	106	38
15–24	2,778	387
25–44	5,721	1,097
25–64	3,671	685
65–74	1,976	269
75+	2,033	124

Source: *World Almanac and Book of Facts, 1994* (Mahwah, NJ: World Almanac, 1993), p. 963.

Among young people who commit suicide, guns are the number one instrument of choice for both boys and girls, responsible for more than six of every ten suicide deaths. Historically, women have relied on poison, but in 1980, there were an estimated 2,600 female suicides by gunshot—39 percent of all female suicides. Only 27 percent of the female suicides used poison.

swimming   When it comes to swimming, women are more energy-efficient than men. The female body has proportionately more fat, so it is more buoyant in the water than a MUSCLE-heavy male body. In addition, a woman's shorter LEGS are positioned higher in the water and propel her body forward more effectively than a man's longer legs. Finally, the extra female body fat acts as an insulator, keeping a woman's body warmer longer in the water and allowing her to conserve energy. Women are less likely to end up chilled on long-distance events in cool waters, such as the English Channel.

But if women win on energy, men pull ahead on speed. Their broad, muscular SHOULDERS and longer ARMS pull them through the water faster, even though their longer, low-lying legs have to work harder at every kick. Because speed swimming records measure styles such as the freestyle, the butterfly, and the breaststroke, all of which rely on arm and shoulder strength, there is not a single category of measured competition swimming in which women come in faster than men. The difference, though small, are real and consistent.

SWIMMING RECORDS MEN VERSUS WOMEN		
Event	**Fastest Male (min:sec)**	**Fastest Female (min:sec)**
Freestyle		
50 meters	0:21.81	0:42.79
100 meters	0:48.42	0:54.48
200 meters	1:46.69	1:57.55
400 meters	3:45.00	4:03.85
800 meters	7:46.60	8:16.22
1,500 meters	14:43.40	15:52.10
Breaststroke		
100 meters	1:01.29	1:07.91
200 meters	2:10.60	2:25.35
Butterfly		
100 meters	0:52.84	0:57.93
200 meters	1:56.57	2:05.90

Source: *The Guinness Book of Records* (New York: Bantam Books, 1994).

systemic lupus erythematosus (SLE)   Systemic lupus erythematosus, more commonly known as lupus, is a potentially fatal long-term inflammatory disorder of the connective tissue. Its most common symptoms are reddened skin and a characteristic butterfly-shaped rash over the nose and cheeks.

Overall, nearly nine of every ten lupus victims are women—most frequently, women younger than 40. Although the exact cause of lupus remains a mystery, there is clearly a hormonal component. Before PUBERTY—that is, before the sex hormones begin to exert their influence—the ratio of girls with lupus to boys with lupus is four to one. In adulthood, it is ten to 15 women for every man. After menopause, it is seven to one.

In addition, lupus worsens when a woman's exposure to estrogen rises, as when she is taking birth control pills or when she is pregnant (lupus patients are at high risk of miscarriage). It is rarely diagnosed for the first time after menopause, when estrogen secretion drops.

T

target areas   Under stress, human beings tend to tense muscles at specific sites in the body. Which muscles tense may depend on genetics and gender.

In 1953, studying world-class athletes under stress conditions to see if their reactions would interfere with their sports performance, scientists in the then–East German city of Leipzig "mapped" their subjects' bodies and discovered that most aimed their stress-related tension at muscles in five spots the researchers labeled "target areas"—the abdomen, the SHOULDERS, the face, the hands, and the lower BACK—as well as a number of miscellaneous target areas, such as the muscles of the larynx, that affect small but significant groups of people.

Since then, researchers have learned that target areas are congenital, sometimes inherited, and often gender-related. Martin Schwartz, research professor in the department of surgery at New York University Medical Center, is the executive director of the National Center for Stuttering, and the man who discovered a target area in the larynx. Schwartz says that women are three times more likely than men to focus stress at the abdominal wall, and therefore three times more likely to develop a "nervous stomach"—more accurately, IRRITABLE BOWEL SYNDROME. Women are also more likely to suffer from pain in the facial muscles caused by tension in the JAW muscles, and pain in the wrist from CARPAL TUNNEL SYNDROME. On the other hand, five times as many men suffer from spasms in the vocal cords; STUTTERING is overwhelmingly a male problem.

Why some target areas should be predominantly female and others predominantly male is a subject rich in theory and speculation based primarily on the behavior of our prehistoric ancestors. Imagine, for example, a Pleistocene couple walking across a meadow. Suddenly, a woolly mammoth rears up in front of

138

them. The woman runs, instinctively protecting a possible fetus. The man stays to fight.

Their instinctive decisions require each to focus energy at specific muscle groups. To run fast, she must tighten her abdominal muscles. To fight effectively, he must tighten his laryngeal muscles, close off his airway, and capture air in his chest, so as to create a rigid fulcrum for his swinging arms. Given the Darwinian principle that only the fittest survive, it's logical to assume that she who runs fastest and he who swings hardest will live to pass their genes—and their abdominal and laryngeal target areas—on to succeeding generations. Unfortunately, the reactions that saved our forbears' lives can make ours miserable. Having buried the instinct for flight or fight, modern men and women end up with knots in the stomach or an emotionally painful stammer.

teeth   One in every 2,000 babies (including Julius Caesar, Louis XIV, Napoleon, and Richard III) is born with at least one tooth, but most of us come toothless into the world and normally sprout our first tooth, a lower central incisor, at about seven and a half months.

This first tooth is one of a set of 20 deciduous ("milk") teeth that appear between the ages of seven months and two years, usually in a fairly standard time sequence. First come the four center incisors ("front teeth"). About three months later, the lateral incisors appear; followed by the canines; and finally, at about 2 ½ years, the second premolars. The first permanent teeth, the molars, show up around age six and remain in place for the rest of a person's life, unless removed because they are impacted (moving up at an angle that prevents them from coming through the gum) or because the jaw is so small that the molars are crowding and displacing other teeth.

Genetics plays a strong role in deciding when the milk teeth and permanent teeth actually appear, says Michael W. Robert, chair of the department of pediatric dentistry at the University of North Carolina School of Dentistry. If Mom and Dad got theirs early (or late), the children are likely to do the same. On average, boys and girls tend to get their first milk teeth at the same time, but girls may lose their baby teeth first and get their first permanent tooth sooner.

The milk teeth are shed between age six and 13. First to go are the incisors, which fall out about a year after the molars begin to push upwards. The replacement of milk teeth with permanent teeth is a steady process. The permanent incisor tooth develops beneath the milk tooth, pushing against the roots of the tooth above it. The pressure produces electrical forces that stimulate special bone-eating cells called osteoclasts to dissolve the legs of the milk tooth; the permanent tooth moves up; and the milk tooth—bereft of its roots—loosens, wiggles, and ultimately falls out, usually with a little help from its owner.

When all the permanent teeth are in, a man's teeth tend to be larger than a woman's. This is so common that it is regarded as one of the most reliable ways to tell whether a skull is male or female.

temperature   Daniel Gabriel Fahrenheit, the inventor of the Fahrenheit scale (in 1714), considered 96 degrees Fahrenheit to be the normal temperature for a healthy adult. In 1878, after reviewing a list of more than one million body temperature readings obtained by pressing a thermometer against the skin of more than 25,000 human armpits, German physician Carl Wunderlich raised "normal" to 98.6 Fahrenheit. (Fahrenheit defined "fever" as any temperature higher than 96 Fahrenheit; Wunderlich raised that, too, to 100.4 Fahrenheit.)

They were both wrong. A small minority of human beings normally run a temperature of 96 Fahrenheit, and about 10 percent of us hit the mark square on at 98.6. But most individuals' normal body temperatures fall somewhere between 96 and 99.9 degrees Fahrenheit, with an average 97.5 degrees Fahrenheit early in the morning, around 6 A.M., rising to an average 98.5 degrees Fahrenheit late in the afternoon, around 4 P.M.

Women are usually slightly warmer than men, but not enough to make a real difference. In 1992, Philip A. Mackowiak and Steven S. Wasserman of the Veterans Affairs Medical Center and the University of Maryland in Baltimore recorded 700 oral temperatures among 148 men and women, age 18 to 40, who had agreed to participate in a trial testing a new vaccine against dysentery. The readings, recorded as often as four times a day for three days by specially trained nurses using electronic thermometers, were a base line against which to judge any reaction after the people in the study had swallowed the experimental vaccine. While the temperatures of individual participants went up and down slightly during the study, the women were a bit warmer, an average 98.4 versus 98.1 for the men. However, a woman's normal body temperature varies during her monthly menstrual cycle, rising about one degree at ovulation and remaining elevated for 11 to 15 days, only to drop back down just before menstrual bleeding begins.

thumb pain   If a thumb aches, the odds are four to one it's a female thumb. So says Robert Lahita, professor of medicine at Cornell University Medical College, who explains that women are four times as likely as men to suffer from rheumatoid arthritis that causes wear and tear on joints, and an aching thumb is a common complaint among older women. CARPAL TUNNEL SYNDROME, a painful disorder of the nerve that controls some movements of the thumb, is also more common among women, perhaps because women are still more likely than men to hold clerical jobs where they are required to use keyboards that require repetitive movements of wrist and hand.

twins   The overwhelming majority of human pregnancies deliver one child from one egg fertilized by one sperm; twins appear once in every 80 pregnancies.

There are two types of twins, identical twins and fraternal twins.[*] Identical twins come from one fertilized egg that has split in two, producing two individuals of the same sex with exactly the same genes and chromosomes. Fraternal twins come from two separate eggs released at the same time and are fertilized by two separate sperm. Fraternal twins are simply siblings, brothers and/or sisters who share some genetic traits and may or may not be of the same sex.

An egg that begins to split but does not complete the job produces conjoined twins, more commonly known as "Siamese twins" after Chang and Eng Bunker, the boys born to Chinese parents in Siam (now Thailand) on May 11, 1811. The brothers, whose names mean "left" and "right" in Thai, lived to be 62, dying within hours of each other on January 17, 1874. To date more than 70 pairs of conjoined twins are recorded in medical literature—more girls than boys, although there is no explanation as to why this should be so.

Men play virtually no role in determining whether any particular conception will produce more than one fetus. Identical twins, say reproductive researchers Richard Naeye and Nebiat Tafari authors of *Risk Factors in Pregnancy and Diseases of the Fetus and Newborn*, are probably "a biologic accident." Because fraternal twins often run in families, releasing more than one egg at a time is probably an inherited characteristic passed along from mother to daughter.

A human pregnancy producing more than two infants is a rare event. Like identical twins, identical triplets, quadruplets and so on come from one fertilized egg that has split into several individuals. The birth rates by gender are similar to all other births, i.e., there are slightly more males. Multiple fetuses from more than one egg are similar to fraternal twins—they are brothers and/or sisters, but not identical. Multiple births of nonidentical children are most common among previously infertile women taking fertility drugs that trigger the release of more than one egg at ovulation.

---

[*]Identical twins are also known as monozygotic twins (mono = one; zygote = fertilized egg); fraternal twins, as dizygotic twins (di = two).

Type A behavior   Classic Type A people are the ones who try to do everything at once. Often, they do a good job of balancing dozens of different tasks and are volubly impatient with slowness in others. They are competitive, even when they don't have to be. They talk fast; interrupt others; and may even finish other people's sentences. Not surprisingly, they are often quick-tempered, compulsive, and hostile.

Their polar opposites are Type B people, the relaxed, less competitive men and women driven neither by time pressures nor by the need to be successful. Nobody really knows whether Type A people are healthier than Type B people, or vice versa, but it is clear that Type A people tend to have higher-than-normal levels of the stress-related hormones sometimes linked to HIGH BLOOD PRESSURE and high serum CHOLESTEROL.

According to Meyer Friedman and Ray Rosenman, the San Francisco heart specialists who named the Type A and Type B syndromes, both men and women may be either Type A or Type B, but there are differences in how they play out their behavioral hands. Women, the doctors say, are more likely to turn their stress reactions inward; men, to lash out in sudden fits of temper. While Type A men are obvious in their stress, Type A women may look incredibly polite and calm while actually seething inside. Whether Type A women will continue to maintain this culturally induced politeness as they move up the ladders of responsibility in business and political life is a matter of some interest.

U

ulcers   Who's most likely to wake up at 1 A.M. with a pain in the gut? The odds are two to one that it's a man. A gnawing pain in the middle of the body in the middle of the night is a common symptom of an ulcer—either a duodenal ulcer (an ulcer in the duodenum—the upper part of the intestinal tract) or a gastric ulcer—an ulcer in the stomach.

A man's risk of a duodenal ulcer is twice as high as a woman's, but his risk of a gastric ulcer is only slightly higher than hers. Female hormones appear to offer some protection. Women with ulcers often find that their symptoms recede while they are pregnant. The continuing male predominance may be particularly interesting to infectious disease specialists because ulcers are now believed to be caused by a bacterium (*Heliobacter pylori*) recently found in drinking water, and bacteria are not notable for favoring one sex over the other.

urinary tract infections   In the United States, urinary tract infections (UTI) are second only to colds and flu as the commonest reason for visiting the doctor.

Women are more susceptible than men to urinary tract infections. Statistical studies put a woman's risk of a urinary infection about ten times higher than a man's, right from childhood. About 5 percent of school-age children develop a urinary tract infection, and starting at age four, the ratio of females to males is at least ten to one. One in every five women will experience a urinary tract infection at some point in her life.

The higher female risk is a product of physiology. A woman's ureter (the tube that runs up from the external urethral opening to the bladder) is nearly seven inches shorter than a man's. As a result, the distance from the female bladder to the anus and the vagina is shorter, and both these areas are richly populated with bacteria.

143

urine   Urine is a waste product composed primarily of water, plus urea and uric acid (products of protein metabolism) and salt. It also contains citric acid and other organic acids, nonprotein nitrogen compounds, sugars, sulfur compounds, minerals (calcium, phosphates, potassium, magnesium), water soluble vitamins, hormones, blood cells, and bacteria, the latter more plentiful in female urine.

The precise amount of each component in a person's urine can vary depending on diet, activity, and stress level. In most cases, the normal ranges are the same for men and women. A few components, however, are gender-related.

The clearest sex differences in urine are the levels of sex hormones, with more estrogen in a woman's urine and more testosterone in a man's. Human chorionic gonadotropin (HCG), a hormone produced by the placenta, is normally found in the urine of pregnant women. When it turns up in the urine of men or of women who are not pregnant, it may be due to cancer of the ovaries or testes, stomach, liver, pancreas, breast, skin (melanoma), or blood (multiple myeloma). Finding pregnanediol, a second placental hormone, in the urine of men or nonpregnant women also suggests cancer—in this case an adrenal tumor—or liver disease, or an obstruction in the ducts leading to or from the gallbladder, the liver, and the pancreas.

Levels of adrenal hormones are also gender-related: 17-hydroxycorticosteroids (17-0HCS) are secreted during the metabolism of hormones that make it possible to convert protein and fat to glucose, which is converted to glycogen, the body's basic fuel; 17-ketogenic steroids (17-KGS), such as cortisol, are produced by the conversion of cholesterol in the cortex (outer layers) of the adrenal gland. Normally, there is more 17-OHCS and 17-KGS in male urine, but levels rise in both men and women when they are subjected to emotional or physical stress.

Creatine and its derivative creatinine are produced when the body metabolizes amino acids, the building blocks of all proteins, including the proteins in foods. How much creatine and creatinine reach the urine depends on how well the substances are filtered by the kidneys. The more efficient the filtration, the lower the level of these two chemicals. Creatine and creatinine are by-products of MUSCLE activity. Because male bodies are proportionately more muscular, male urine levels of these two substances are higher.

Hydroxyproline is an amino acid found in collagen, a component of skin and BONE. Hydroxyproline levels rise in urine when a bone breaks, during periods of rapid bone growth such as adolescence, or when a person has a disorder such as OSTEOPOROSIS characterized by bone resorption. Ordinarily, there is slightly more hydroxyproline in male urine. A woman's hydroxyproline levels go up during the last trimester of PREGNANCY, when the fetal SKELETON is growing rapidly.

Porphyrins are red-orange pigments produced during the synthesis of heme, a red pigment in blood cells that carries oxygen throughout the body. Normally, a woman's porphyrin levels are higher than a man's. In both sexes, elevated levels point to impaired heme synthesis or liver disease due to a genetic defect or a blood disorder such as PORPHYRIA.

Urobilogen is what's left after intestinal bacteria digest bilirubin, a red pigment in bile. The level of urobilogen in a healthy woman's urine may be twice that in a healthy man's, but urobilogen levels rise when there is an obstruction of the biliary system, such as a tumor in one of the ducts leading to or from the liver, the gallbladder, or the pancreas.

URINE TESTS WITH GENDER-RELATED RESULTS

Substance	Male	Female (adult)	Female (postmenopause)
Arylsulfatase	1.4–19.3 units/L	1.4–11 units/L	
Creatinine	1–1.9 g/day[*]	0.8–1.7 g/day	
Estrogens	4–25 mcg/day	5–100 mcg/day	
17-hydroxy-corticosteroids (17-0HCS)	4.5–12 mg/day	2.5–10 mg/day	
Hydroxyproline	0.4–5 mg/2 hr	0.4–2.9 mg/2 hr[**]	
17-ketogenicsteroids (17-KGS)	4–14 mg/day	2–12 mg/day	
Porphyrins	0–42 mcg/day	1–22 mg/day	
Testosterone	up to 200 200 mcg/day	not more than 10 mcg/day	
Urobilogen	0.3–2.1 Erlich units /2 hrs	0.1–1.1 Erlich units /2 hrs	

[*]Some values are measured in one urine sample; others, such as this, are measured in samples collected in a large container over a full 24-hour day.

[**]Values may rise during third trimester of pregnancy, indicating growth of fetal skeleton. Levels rise when bone is being reabsorbed and in periods of rapid bone growth, i.e. among children and adolescents.

Sources: *Diagnostic Tests Handbook*, ed. Regina Daley Ford (Springhouse, PA: Springhouse Corporation, 1986); Cathey Pinckney and Edward R. Pinckney, *The Patient's Guide to Medical Tests* (New York: Facts On File, 1984).

URINE FLOW			
Age	Min. vol. (ml)	Male (ml/sec)	Female (ml/sec)
4–7 yr.	100	10	10
8–13	100	12	15
14–45	200	21	18
46–65	200	12	15
66–80	200	9	10

Source: *Diagnostic Tests Handbook*, ed. Regina Daley Ford (Springhouse, PA: Springhouse Corporation, 1988), p. 660.

urine, flow rate   How much urine the body makes is an overall guide to its fluid balance. The speed and volume of the urine stream—the flow rate—is an indication of the overall health of the urinary tract.

Under ordinary circumstances, healthy adults void between 700 and 2,000 ml of urine a day. To measure flow rate, the doctor directs the patient to urinate into a funnel that measures the amount of urine and shows how quickly it flows. A higher-than-normal flow rate suggests a reduction of tension in the urethral sphincter, the muscles that circle the urethral opening. A lower-than-normal flow rate may indicate an obstruction in the urethra or a tightening of the sphincter muscles. Among adults aged 14 to 45, men produce more urine and their urine flows faster, so men's flow rate is normally higher than women's.

V

varicose veins   A woman's BLOOD VESSELS are more expandable than a man's. This hormone-related effect is strongest during the reproductive years, when women are at lower risk of HIGH BLOOD PRESSURE. As a result, women are four times more likely than men to suffer from varicose veins, with varicosities likely to be larger and more uncomfortable. This is especially true during pregnancy, when a woman's body produces hormones that relax ligaments in muscles, including the smooth muscle in the walls of the uterus and the blood vessels. The relaxed uterus stretches to hold the developing fetus; the relaxed blood vessels expand to accommodate an increased supply of blood to the fetus. Sometimes, the expansion of the blood vessels weakens internal valves designed to keep blood from flowing backward, down into veins in the legs. When the blood pools, the veins swell. The good news is that after delivery the valves are likely to return to normal so that many varicosities shrink or disappear entirely.

vitamin A   Vitamin A is essential for vision, growth, and reproduction. It facilitates the reproduction and growth of cells and maintains the immune system.

Our bodies derive vitamin A from two different types of compounds in food; retinoids and carotenoids. Retinoids, such as retinol, retinaldehyde, and retinoic acid, are found in animal products including eggs and milk. Carotenoid precursors such as beta-carotene and alpha-carotene are found in plants, such as spinach, and in some animal fats. Vitamin A dissolves in fat: retinoids are stored in the liver, carotenoids in body fat and the adrenal glands. Because women have more body fat, they store vitamin A more efficiently.

Originally, vitamin A values were described in terms of international units (IU), with 1 IU equal to 0.30 micrograms of retinal acetate or 0.60 micrograms

---

GOOD SOURCES OF VITAMIN A

Food Portions That Provide 40 Percent of the RDA for Adults and Children Older Than Four

Oatmeal, instant, fortified	2/3 cup
Mango	½ medium
Carrots, cooked	½ cup
Carrots, raw	4 3" strips
Kale, cooked	½ cup
Peas and carrots, cooked	½ cup
Pepper, sweet red	1 small
Spinach, cooked	½ cup
Sweet potato	1 medium
Turnip greens, cooked	½ cup
Liver	3 ounces

Source: *Good Sources of Nutrients* (Washington, D.C.: USDA, Human Nutrition Services, January 1990).

---

of beta-carotene. But advances in nutritional research showed that similar amounts of different carotenoids may provide different amounts of vitamin A. That discovery has led to a more accurate and convenient unit of measurement for vitamin A, the retinol equivalent (RE), the real-life portion of food that provides an amount of vitamin A equal to one microgram of retinol.

The recommended dietary allowances for vitamin A, based on average body weight, are 1,000 RE for a healthy adult man and 800 RE for a healthy adult woman. Women who are nursing require an additional 500 RE during the first six months of lactation and an additional 400 RE during the second six months.

vitamin B complex   The B vitamin complex includes several very different compounds originally thought to be one vitamin, but eventually isolated, identified, and defined as thiamine, riboflavin, niacin, vitamin B6, folate, and vitamin B12.

The members of the vitamin B complex do have a lot in common. They are all water soluble, easy to absorb, and relatively nontoxic at high levels. They all act as coenzymes—partners with enzymes in digesting food and facilitating reactions among cells in every part of the body. Except for vitamin B12, which is found only in foods of animal origin, they are all available in organ meats, poultry, fish, grains, nuts and seeds, and some fruits and vegetables, but they are easily destroyed when food is stored, processed, or cooked.

As a rule, the recommended dietary allowances (RDA) for members of the vitamin B complex are determined by the amount of food a person eats in an

VITAMIN B COMPLEX RECOMMENDED DIETARY ALLOWANCES

Gender/Age	Thiamin (mg)	Riboflavin (mg)	Niacin (mg)	Vitamin B6 (mg)	Folate (mcg)	Vitamin B12 (mcg)
Women						
11–14 yrs.	1.1	1.3	15	1.4	150	2.0
15–18 yrs.	1.1	1.3	15	1.5	180	2.0
19–50 yrs.	1.1	1.3	15	1.6	180	2.0
51+	1.0	1.2	13	1.6	180	2.0
Pregnant	1.5	1.6	17	2.2	400	2.2
Nursing	1.6	1.8	20	2.1	280	2.6
Men						
11–14 yrs.	1.3	1.5	17	1.7	150	2.0
15–18 yrs.	1.5	1.8	20	2.0	200	2.0
19–50 yrs.	1.5	1.7	19	2.0	200	2.0
51+	1.2	1.4	15	2.0	200	2.0

Source: National Research Council, *Recommended Dietary Allowances*, 10th ed. (Washington, D.C.: National Academy Press, 1989).

average day. Because men ordinarily eat more than women, their RDAs are slightly higher. However, there are two specific instances when women need larger amounts of B vitamins: when they are using birth control pills (which appear to lower blood levels of vitamin B6) and when they are pregnant. By taking 400 mg of folate a day early in pregnancy, a woman appears to cut in half her child's risk of a neural tube defect such as spina bifida. In 1992, the Public Health Service issued a recommendation that all women of childbearing age take folic acid supplements, and a review panel of experts at the Food and Drug Administration recommended fortifying foods with folic acid. But the recommendation has not been implemented because of concerns about the risks of universal vitamin therapy, particularly for elderly Americans, in whom large doses of folic acid might mask the symptoms of another B vitamin deficiency.

vitamin C   The recommended dietary allowance for vitamin C is the same for men and women—a daily intake of 60 mg to prevent a deficiency in vitamin C that leads to the disease scurvy. During pregnancy the requirement rises to 70 mg a day. A pregnant woman who smokes requires even more; smoking appears to reduce the amount of vitamin C in a pregnant woman's blood by at least 15 percent. In the first six months of nursing, the requirement increases further, to 95 mg a day; in the the second six months, it drops back to 90 mg a day. (See table on page 151.)

GOOD SOURCES OF B VITAMINS

Food Portions That Provide 10–24 Percent of the RDA for Adults and Children Older Than Four

Note: 1 ounce of cold cereal (fortified) provides 10–24 percent of every B vitamin except vitamin B12.

Thiamine
Pork	3 ounces
Sunflower seeds, hulled, unroasted	2 tablespoons

Riboflavin
Yogurt, lowfat	8 ounces
Liver	2 ounces

Niacin
Chicken, without skin	3 ounces
Lamb	1 chop
Liver	3 ounces
Veal	3 ounces
Mackerel, mullet, salmon, swordfish	3 ounces

Vitamin B6
Banana	1 medium

Folate
Spinach, cooked	½ cup
Beef	3 ounces
Pork	2 ounces
Chicken, cooked, diced	½ cup

Vitamin B12
Beef, lean	3 ounces
Catfish, perch, pike, salmon, swordfish	3 ounces
Clams, crabmeat, lobster, mackerel, mussels, trout, tuna	2 ounces

Source: *Good Sources of Nutrients* (Washington, D.C.: USDA, Human Nutrition Services, January 1990).

---

vitamin D   Vitamin D is essential for the absorption of calcium; it plays a significant role in building strong bones and teeth. The recommended dietary allowance (RDA) is the same for men and women—400 IU a day; for women older than 24, the requirement is 200 IU higher during pregnancy or while nursing. In the United States, milk is fortified with Vitamin D. Our bodies also manufacture vitamin D when we are exposed to sunlight.

GOOD SOURCES OF VITAMIN C

Food Portions That Provide 25–39 Percent of the RDA for Adults and Children Older Than Four

Apple, grape, grapefruit, orange, pineapple, and tomato juice	¾ cup
Cantaloupe, mandarin orange sections, peaches, pineapple, raspberries (unsweetened)	½ cup
Artichoke, banana, kiwi fruit, nectarine, orange, pear, plantain, plum, pomegranate, sweet potato	1 medium

Source: *Good Sources of Nutrients* (Washington, D.C.: USDA, Human Nutrition Services, January 1990).

vitamin E   Vitamin E is made up of related compounds called tocopherols. Tocopherols are antioxidants. They trap and inactivate free radicals—molecules that would otherwise create potentially destructive substances in the body. In the body, tocopherols are secreted from the liver on very low density LIPOPROTEINS (VLDLs), then transferred to either low density lipoproteins (LDLs), the "bad" fat and protein particles that carry CHOLESTEROL into arteries, or high density

GOOD SOURCES OF VITAMIN E

Food Portions That Provide 10–24 Percent of the RDA for Adults and Children Older Than Four

Multigrain cereal, cooked	2/3 cup
Apple, baked	1 medium
Apricots, canned	½ cup
Nectarine	1 medium
Peaches, canned	½ cup
Greens (chard, dandelion, kohlrabi, mustard, turnip), cooked	½ cup
Pumpkin, cooked	½ cup
Shellfish (clams, scallops, shrimp), boiled, broiled, canned	3 ounces
Fish (mackerel, mullet, ocean perch, salmon)	3 ounces
Peanut butter	1 tablespoon
Nuts and seeds	1–2 tablespoons

Source: *Good Sources of Nutrients* (Washington, D.C.: USDA, Human Nutrition Services, January 1990).

lipoproteins (HDLs), the "good" particles that carry cholesterol out of the body. In women, more cholesterol is carried on HDLs than on LDLs, but blood concentrations of tocopherol are similar for men and women.

The recommended dietary allowance (RDA) for vitamin E, based on average body weight, is 10 mg Alpha-TE for a man and 8 mg α–TE for a woman. During pregnancy, the RDA is 10 mg α-TE; while nursing, 11–12 mg αTE

vocal cords   At birth, a baby's vocal cords are about one-quarter inch long. They grow longer as the body grows heavier and taller, but until PUBERTY, they grow at equal rates in boys and girls. At age two, the vocal cords are one-third inch long; at age six, four-tenths of an inch; at age ten, one-half inch.

Things change quickly at adolescence, when a boy's vocal cords begin to grow faster and longer than a girl's. Given his longer vocal cords, a teenage boy should have a VOICE that is consistently lower and deeper than a girl's. Instead, the adolescent male voice rises and falls, scratches and cracks, as a boy struggles to control the muscles surrounding his larynx, which also enlarges at puberty, forming the "ADAM'S APPLE."

The male voice begins to crack just about the time that penis development ends. That is why early church choirs, seeking to retain their soprano voices, castrated boys in the late teens. Church records show that 200 years ago the average age at which boys' voices changed was about 18; today, it may be as early as 13.

By age 20, the male lanryngeal muscles are under control. A young man's vocal cords are now about an inch long, one-third inch longer than a young woman's, and his voice is deeper. At age 30, the difference is even more pronounced. Now the male vocal cords are about 1.25 inches long, the female vocal cords three-quarters of an inch. The extra half inch is enough to create a distinct, recognizable vocal difference between the sexes that will last straight through the reproductive years. Among the elderly, the length of the vocal cords changes for the last time. The vocal cords grow shorter, and both male and female voices rise in pitch, becoming thin and reedy with age.

voice   Whether a human voice is high or low, soprano or bass, depends on the length of the VOCAL CORDS. The longer the cords, the lower the pitch. Because male vocal cords are generally longer than female vocal cords, male voices are usually lower in pitch.

The high or low tones in the voice also depend on frequency—the number of times a sound wave vibrates in a given period of time, expressed as cycles per second. The sound of middle C vibrates at a frequency of 256 cycles per second. The basic tone of the human voice is about 125 cycles per second. The frequency for an average male voice is lower than that for an average female voice.

Pitch and frequency are clearly gender-related characteristics. Resonance, the sound of the voice vibrating in the body's "resonating chambers"—mouth, throat, chest—may or may not be gender-related. As a rule, the male body offers larger resonating chambers, so the male voice generally sounds more powerful. But there are plentiful exceptions to this rule, as anyone who has ever sat through a Wagnerian opera starring a barrel-chested soprano knows.

The final measure of a voice is volume, the loudness or softness—a shout versus a whisper. Despite differences in pitch and resonance, men and women seem able, if pushed, to be equally loud. The loudest shout ever recorded for a woman was 18-year-old Annalisa Wray's 119.4 decibel bellow at the International Rally Arura in Coleraine, Northern Ireland on August 11, 1992. The loudest recorded shout for a man was Bermudan Donald H. Burns's slightly quieter 119 decibel yell four years earlier, on January 19, 1989, at Liberty State Park in New Jersey. By way of comparison, a soft whisper from a person standing five meters away registers 30 decibels; average conversation is 65 decibels; a pneumatic drill registers 115 decibels; a jet aircraft taking off, 130.

W

walking   A man's PELVIS is narrower than a woman's in relation to his body. His HIPS are closer together and so are his legs, which come down straight to the ground, so that to walk forward, he has only to move his legs up and down.

A woman's wider pelvis and broader hips push her legs further apart and turn them outward at a slight angle. In order to move forward, she has to move her thighs in a slight but definite half-circle, the motion that makes hips and buttocks swing in the characteristic female gait.

A man's legs are usually longer than a woman's, which gives him a longer stride, allowing him to move forward faster. The female speed record for a 10 kilometer walk—41 minutes 56.23 seconds, set by Nadezhda Ryashkina in Seattle, Washington on July 24, 1990—is nearly four minutes longer than the male record of 38 minutes 2.6 seconds, set by Jozef Pribiliner of Czechoslovakia in Banski Bystrica on August 30, 1985.

water   The human body is 50 percent to 70 percent water. Because there is more water in MUSCLE tissue than in fat and because men have proportionately more muscle, their bodies contain more water [see BODY COMPOSITION]. As a result, men can drink more ALCOHOL before showing ill effects; the additional water in their tissues dilutes the alcohol more efficiently.

On an average day, when the air temperature is neither too hot nor too cold, an average 150-pound man excretes about 2,400 ml* of water through urination, defecation, respiration, and PERSPIRATION—a loss of 1 ml of water for every CALORIE spent. Some of this lost fluid will be replaced with water from food—a raw apple, for example, is 84 percent water; a 100 mg/3.5 ounce lean hamburger is 56 percent water. Water is also replenished from the water molecules created

---

*30 ml = 1 ounce

as a by-product of metabolism. But most of the water the body needs is supplied by fluids; in fact, the standard old wives' recommendation of eight 10-ounce glasses a day will supply precisely the 2,400 ml the average man requires.

When a person exercises, does physical work, or spends time in a place where the temperature is high, breathing quickens and perspiration increases, and the body loses water faster. As a rule of thumb, to avoid dehydration it is necessary to add one milliliter of water for every extra calorie spent. For example, a sedentary adult male spends about 2,400 calories in the course of an average day. If he starts to exercise and increases his energy expenditure by 1,500 calories, to 3,900 calories a day, he needs to increase his fluid consumption by 1,500 ml—the amount of water in five 10-ounce glasses of water. It usually takes anywhere from 30 minutes to an hour to absorb eight ounces of water into the body from the stomach and intestines.

Pregnant women need extra liquids to accommodate the normal increase in blood volume and fluid between the cells, as well as the amniotic fluid surrounding the fetus. The National Research Council recommends an additional 1,000 ml water a day for a nursing mother who secretes an average 750 ml of milk each day.

weight   At birth, boys weigh slightly more than girls, and with the exception of the few short years during puberty when girls develop faster and grow more quickly than boys, males generally weigh more than females.

The usual assumption is that this weight difference is due to the male body's heavier bones and bulkier MUSCLES, but the difference between men and women of equal height, while real, is small. For example, as Anthony Smith points out in *The Body*, a five-foot-tall woman may weigh only five pounds less than a five-foot-tall man, a six-foot-tall woman only six pounds less than a six-foot-tall man. Therefore, Smith says, most of the difference in male and female weight is due simply to the fact that men are usually taller [see HEIGHT].

The greatest median weight for an adult American man, 174 pounds, occurs sometime between age 24 and 50. The greatest median weight for an adult American woman is 143 pounds, sometime after age 51. After this, as they grow older both men and women lose bone mass, muscle mass, and weight.

The heaviest person whose weight was reliably recorded was a man named Jon Brower Minnoch. Minnoch, who was born in Bainbridge Island, Washington, in 1941, was overweight from the time he was a child. In 1978, he was estimated to weigh nearly 1,400 pounds when he was admitted to University Hospital, Seattle, at the age of 37, suffering from heart failure and respiratory distress. At the time of his death in September 1983, after more than 16 months on a liquid diet, Minnoch weighed 798 pounds. The heaviest woman on record is Rosalie Bradford, who weighed in at 1,050 pounds in January 1987 when she was 47.

white blood cells   White blood cells are made and stored in bone marrow and spleen as well as in the thymus and lymph glands. They are an integral part of the body's IMMUNE SYSTEM, helping to fight infection by engulfing and destroying the organisms that cause disease and inflammation. On average, boys have slightly more white blood cells than girls do, but in adulthood, the normal range for white blood cells is exactly the same for men and women, 4,100–10,900 per microliter of blood.

wrinkles   Wrinkles suggest that a face is female. There are two reasons why this should be so. First, a woman's SKIN is thinner than a man's. Second, her SEBACEOUS GLANDS are not as efficient later in life.

Skin is composed of several layers of cells. The top layer, the epidermis, is equal in depth in men and women, but the dermis, the second layer of skin cells, is microscopically thicker in male skin. With age, everybody's dermis thins and sags, but because the male dermis starts out thicker, a man's skin stays thicker and firmer longer. In addition, an older man's sebaceous glands continue to secrete normal amounts of sebum to lubricate the skin longer than an older woman's. Therefore, a woman's skin generally wrinkles earlier than a man's.

X

X-linked traits   An X-linked trait is a BIRTH DEFECT or inherited characteristic transmitted via a gene carried on the X chromosome. X-linked traits are also known as sex-linked traits because they affect men more often and more severely than women.

While still in the embryonic stage, a female experiences a phenomenon called X chromosome inactivation. As a result, one of the two X chromosomes in every female body cell is inactivated, to remain nonfunctional forever. The process is random; there is no way of knowing which X chromosome will be inactivated in any given cell. If a male inherits an X chromosome with a gene for a sex-linked defect, that gene will be present in every cell in his body. But if a female inherits an X chromosome with the "bad" gene, on average, the chromosome will be inactivated in half the cells in her body and its effects will therefore be lessened.

For example, a man who inherits an X chromosome with the gene for FABRY'S DISEASE (a rare enzyme deficiency that allows fatty substances to build up in arteries) will invariably suffer skin lesions, kidney failure, and heart attack, but a woman who carries the gene (and can pass it on to her children) may not show any signs of illness.

All X-linked disorders have several things in common. First, they are transmitted from mothers to sons, but never from fathers to sons (fathers pass only Y chromosomes to their sons). Second, both mother and father may transmit a sex-linked trait to their daughters through their X chromosomes. However, except in those rare instances in which a daughter inherits the gene from both parents, the girls (who become carriers) will escape its serious effects (see above). Third, not every woman who passes a sex-linked trait to her son is a true carrier; in some cases, the gene is defective due to a spontaneous mutation. Fourth, a father carrying an X-linked gene will transmit it to all his daughters

157

but none of his sons. A woman carrying the gene will give it to half her daughters and half her sons. When the mother is a carrier and the father has the trait, half the sons and all the daughters will get the gene. Fifth, if the defect is severe enough, the affected males are unlikely to survive to reproductive age, and the genetic chain is broken. For example, boys with Duchenne MUSCULAR DYSTRO-PHY rarely live long enough to have children of their own.

Y

yeast infections *Candida albicans* is a yeast commonly found in the mouth, the vagina, and the feces of healthy people. Ordinarily, it is kept in check by competing microorganisms, but when the body's defenses are compromised—for example, by DIABETES, long-term antibiotic treatment, or an immune deficiency disease such as AIDS—*Candida* may begin to grow out-of-control. The result is a yeast infection, usually in the warm, moist folds of the body such as the spaces between the toes or in the creases of the legs and buttocks ("diaper rash"). Among adults, genital yeast infections are more common in women, but men may also suffer yeast infection at the tip or underside of the penis, particularly if their female sexual partners have vaginal yeast infections. Persistent yeast infections of the mouth and throat, known as "thrush," may be a symptom of HIV INFECTION.

Z

zinc   Zinc is essential for life. It is a constituent of enzymes that run most of the body's major metabolic processes and is intimately involved in maintaining a healthy male reproductive system. Zinc is stored in muscle and bone. Because men have more muscle tissue and larger bones, they also have larger stores of zinc, the largest supply being in the testes.

Zinc protects the health of the prostate gland and contributes to the production of testosterone; it is vital to sperm production and sexual desire. Even a mild zinc deficiency may lead to reduced sperm counts; a moderate deficiency might reduce the sex drive; a severe deficiency may result in shrunken testes and dwarfism. (Studies on laboratory animals show that zinc deficiency in pregnant females may result in offspring with developmental disorders.)

GOOD SOURCES OF ZINC

Food Portions That Provide 10–24 Percent of the RDA for Adults and Children Older Than Four

Beef, lean	3 ounces
Liver (beef, pork)	3 ounces
Liver (calf)	2 ounces
Liver (chicken)	½ cup
Tongue	3 ounces
Veal, lean	3 ounces
Oysters	2 ounces
Nuts and seeds	4 tablespoons
Yogurt, plain	16 ounces

Source: *Good Sources of Nutrients* (Washington, D.C.: USDA, Human Nutrition Services, January 1990).

Just as women lose iron when they menstruate, men lose zinc when they ejaculate. Those who are extremely active sexually should pay heed to the National Research Council's recommended dietary allowance (RDA)—15 mg for healthy adult males, 12 mg a day for healthy adult females.

Zinc may come from either food or supplements. About 70 percent of dietary zinc comes from animal products, including meat (particularly liver), eggs, and seafood. The recommended dietary allowances are 15 mg for men; 12 mg for women.

Notes and References

accidents: Head trauma and car accidents, *The Merck Manual*, 16th ed., ed. Robert Berkow (Rahway, NJ: Merck, Sharpe & Dohme, 1992), p. 1114.

achondroplasia: *The Merck Manual*, 16th ed., op. cit., p. 2074, p. 2288; Laurence E. Karp, "Older fathers and genetic mutations," *American Journal of Medical Genetics*, 1980.

acne: Response to male hormones, "Skin Care Supplement," *US Pharmacist*, June 1993; incidence statistics, Joye Ann Billow, "Acne care products," *Handbook of Nonprescription Drugs*, 9th ed. (Washington, D.C.: American Pharmaceutical Association, 1990), page 794; older women, Albert M. Kligman, Gary L. Grove, Arthur K. Balin, "The Aging of Human Skin," *Handbook of the Biology of Aging*, 2nd ed. (New York: Van Nostrand Reinhold, 1985)

aging: See Beard, Blood Pressure, etc.

AIDS: 17 percent increase in incidence, "AIDS cases rising sharply among women," *New York Times*, February 10, 1995; transmission of HIV virus, "AIDS is now the leading killer of Americans from 25 to 44," *New York Times*, January 31, 1995.

alcohol, effects on reproduction: "Brewer's droop," interview with Arthur L. Barnett, M.D., Johns Hopkins Hospital; "Paternal alcohol use and fetal development," Rush-Presbyterian–St. Luke's Medical Center *Insights*, vol. 14, no. 2, 1991; "Cocaine may piggyback on sperm into egg," *Science News*, October 1991; E. J. Waterson et al., 1990.

alcohol, tolerance for: Muscles, fat and water, *U.S. Pharmacist*, March 1985; Lieber studies of alcohol dehydrogenase, "Study tells why alcohol is greater risk to women," *New York Times*, January 11, 1990; "Barroom biology: How alcohol goes to a woman's head," *New York Times*, January 14, 1990; Mario Frezza et al., "High blood alcohol levels in women," *The New England Journal of Medicine*, January 11, 1990; Rolando Hernendez-Munoz et al., "Human gastric alcohol dehydrogenase: Its inhibition by H2-receptor antagonists and its effect on the bioavailability of ethanol," *Alcoholism: Clinical and Experimental Research*, November–December 1990; timing of liver enzyme secretion, Kenneth Jon Rose, *The Body in Time* (New York: John Wiley & Sons, 1988), p. 87; Buffalo, New York study, "Women drinking alcohol: When less is more," *Science News*, November 19, 1994.

altitude: Altitude sickness, *The Merck Manual*, 16th ed., op. cit., pp. 2536–37; city altitudes, *The World Almanac and Book of Facts, 1994* (Mahwah, NJ: World Almanac, 1993), pp. 262–63; Spanish conquistadors, Rose, *The Body in Time*, op. cit., p. 17.

Alzheimer's disease: California study, University of California–San Francisco press release, December 2, 1987; Sherwin study, *New York Times*, March 8, 1994.

amyotrophic lateral sclerosis: *Harrison's Principles of Internal Medicine*, 12th ed., ed. Jean D. Wilson et. al. (New York: McGraw-Hill, 1991), p. 2072; *The Merck Manual*, 16th ed., op. cit., pp. 1512–13.

ankylosing spondylitis: *Stedman's Medical Dictionary*, 26th ed., (Baltimore: Williams & Wilkins, 1995).

anorexia nervosa: Causes, *The Merck Manual*, 16th ed., op. cit., p. 2279; Rochester study, *Current Medical Diagnosis and Treatment*, ed. Lawrence M. Tierney Jr. et al. (East Norwalk, CT: Appleton & Lange, 1993), p. 971; Jane E. Brody, "Personal Health," *New York Times*, May 19, 1988; 20 years' knowledge of other problems, Anne Scott Beller, *Fat and Thin* (New York: Farrar, Straus & Giroux, 1977), p. 224; British study, alternative explanations, Alexandra W. Logue, *The Psychology of Eating and Drinking* (New York: W. H. Freeman, 1986), p. 161, p. 165.

Apert's syndrome: *Stedman's Medical Dictionary*, op. cit.; Laurence E. Karp, "Older fathers and genetic mutations," op. cit.

appendicitis: Puberty to age 25–30, *Harrison's Principles of Internal Medicine*, 12th ed., op. cit., p. 1298, and *Current Medical Diagnosis and Treatment 1993*, op. cit., p. 486; incidence statistics, *Mayo Clinic Health Letter*, February 1987; laxatives, *The Merck Manual*, 5th ed., 1923; no laxatives, *The Merck Manual*, 6th ed., 1934; discovery of infection, A. S. E. Ackermann, *Popular Fallacies Explained and Corrected*, 3rd ed. (Philadelphia: Lippincott, 1928), p. 204.

arm: Length, Anthony Smith, The Body (New York: Viking, 1986), Smith, *The Body*, p. 504; hormones and relative strength, Michael Hutchison, "Sex on the brain," *Playboy*, n.d.; shoulder and chest, *Harrison's Principles of Internal Medicine*, 12th ed., op. cit., p. 1769.

arthritis: Incidence, *Arthritis Today*, January–February 1994; and *The Merck Manual*, 16th ed., op. cit., p. 1305, p. 1334; pregnancy effects, *American Health*, January–February 1994.

asthma: Gerald B. Merenstein, David W. Kaplan, Adam A. Rosenberg, *Handbook of Pediatrics*, 16th ed. (Norwalk, CT: Appleton & Lange, 1991), p. 948; *Harrison's Principles of Internal Medicine*, 12th ed., op. cit., p. 1047.

athlete's foot: *Handbook of Pediatrics*, op. cit., p. 558; Nicholas G. Popovich, "Foot care products," *Handbook of Nonprescription Drugs*, 9th ed. (Washington, D.C.: American Pharmaceutical Association, 1990), p. 978.

back: See muscle, perspiration.

baldness: Aristotle quote, Smith, *The Body*, op. cit., p. 247, p. 248; one-third figure, American Academy of Dermatology news release, November 15, 1994; genetics, *Harrison's Principles of Internal Medicine*, 12th ed., op. cit., p. 30.

basal metabolism: National Research Council, *Recommended Dietary Allowances*, 10th ed. (Washington, D.C.: National Research Council, 1989); USDA study, *USDA Quarterly Report*, January–February 1993.

beard: Changes in old age, ethnicity of female facial hair, Kligman et al., *Handbook of the Biology of Aging*, 2nd ed., op. cit.; hirsutism, *Current Medical Diagnosis and Treatment*, op. cit., pp. 893–94.

bed-wetting: Incidence in children, Markku Partinen, "Epidemiology of sleep disorders," *Principles and Practices of Sleep Medicine*, 2nd ed., ed. Meir

Kryger et al. (Philadelphia: W. B. Saunders, 1994); incidence at various ages, *The Merck Manual*, 16th ed., op. cit., p. 2097; boys control bladders later, Merenstein et al., *Handbook of Pediatrics*, 16th ed., op. cit., p. 350; bed-wetting among older children, *The Columbia University College of Physicians and Surgeons Complete Home Medical Guide*, revised ed., ed. Donald F. Tapley et al. (New York: Crown Publishers, 1989), p. 766; Danish research, "Bedwetting traced to genetic flaw," *Science News*, August 12, 1995.

birth, premature: *The Merck Manual*, 16th ed., op. cit., p. 1972; *Man's Body*, ed. The Diagram Group (New York: Bantam Books, 1981), pp. A05–06.

birth defects: Number of birth defects, The March of Dimes Foundation, January 1993; older parents, J. M. Friedman, "Genetic disease in the offspring of older fathers," *Obstetrics & Gynecology*, June 1981; interview with Friedman, 1995; Laurence E. Karp, "Older fathers and genetic mutations," op. cit.; X-linked birth defects, see individual entries.

birth weight: Newborn weight at 5 percent of mother's weight, testosterone effects, Richard L. Naeye and Nebiat Tafari, *Risk Factors in Pregnancy and Diseases of the Fetus and Newborn* (Baltimore: Williams & Wilkins, 1983); average weight at 7.4 lb., *Man's Body*, op. cit., pp. A05–06.

bladder cancer: *Cancer Facts & Figures 1995* (New York: The American Cancer Society, 1994).

blood flow: Mayo Clinic study, "Another male/female difference," *Science News*, November 29, 1986; interview, John Cooke.

blood groups: Number of blood groups, Xg group, *Stedman's Medical Dictionary*, 26th ed., op. cit., and 24th ed.; explanation of sex-linked transmission, *Columbia University College of Physicians and Surgeons Complete Home Medical Guide*, revised ed., op. cit., p. 577.

blood poisoning: Definition, *Stedman's Medical Dictionary*, 26th ed., op. cit.; statistics, The National Center for Health Statistics, "Vital Statistics of the United States, 1991" (Washington, D.C.: U.S. Public Health Service, 1994).

blood tests: Blood values and test descriptions, Cathey Pinckney and Edward R. Pinckney, *The Patient's Guide to Medical Tests* (New York: Facts On File,

1978); and *Diagnostic Tests Handbook*, ed. Regina Daley Ford (Springhouse, PA: Springhouse Corporation, 1986).

blood vessels: Janet Landau, Varicose veins, *U.S. Pharmacist*, July 1989; changes in pregnancy, *The Merck Manual*, 16th ed., op. cit., p. 590; and interview, Ronald Dee, Albert Einstein College of Medicine, New York.

blood volume: Increased female capacity during pregnancy, increased blood volume, male vs. female fetus, Naeye and Tafari, *Risk Factors in Pregnancy and Diseases of the Fetus and Newborn*, op. cit., p. 314–315.

body composition: Percentage of fat, Logue, *The Psychology of Eating and Drinking*, op. cit., p. 165; muscle weight, Smith, *The Body*, op. cit., p. 506; fat vs. muscle tissue, National Research Council, *Recommended Dietary Allowances*, 10th ed., op. cit., pp. 24–31 passim; alcohol, see *alcohol, tolerance for.*

body odor: Complex chemicals in underarm sweat, "Secrets of body odor revealed; may lead to better deodorants," American Chemical Society press release, August 17, 1990; underarm sweat, male/female scents, Natalie Angier, "There is only one scent of a woman and a man," *New York Times*, February 14, 1995; age and perspiration, Kligman et al., "Aging of Human Skin," *Handbook of the Biology of Aging*, 2nd ed., op. cit., pp. 825–27; composition of deodorants, antiperspirants, Donald R. Miller, Mary Kuzel, "Personal care products," *Handbook of Nonprescription Drugs*, 9th ed., op. cit., p. 754.

body shape: Interview with Ruben Andres, U.S. Dept. of Aging, 1987; apple/pear shapes, fat receptors, "Body shape: In the eye of the receptors," *Science News*, January 23, 1988; general male/female bodies, clothing sizes, Beller, *Fat and Thin*, op. cit., pp. 63–64.

bones: Types of bone, National Research Council, *Recommended Dietary Allowances*, 10th ed., op. cit., p. 174; comparative bone densities, incidence of disease, "Prevention and treatment of osteoporosis in women," *U.S. Pharmacist*, supplement, September 1994; rate of fractures, Osteoporosis Fact Sheet, National Osteoporosis Foundation (n.d.).

brain: Size, weight, *The Visual Dictionary of the Human Body* (New York: Dorling Kindersley, 1991); water, Smith, *The Body*, op. cit., p. 337; brain records, *The Guinness Book of Records*, ed. Peter Matthews (New York: Bantam Books, 1994), p. 169; age-related changes, *The New York Times*, April 2, 1991.

brain cells: Number of cells, *The Visual Dictionary of the Human Body*, op. cit., and Simon LeVay, *The Sexual Brain* (Cambridge, MA: MIT Press, 1994), pp. 99–100; "Man's world, woman's world? Brain studies point to differences," *New York Times*, February 28, 1995.

breast: Drugs that cause breast enlargement, James W. Long and James J. Rybacki, *The Essential Guide to Prescription Drugs, 1995* (New York: Harper-Collins, 1994); *Physician's Desk Reference*, 48th ed. (Montvale, NJ: Medical Economics Data Production Company, 1994).

breast cancer: Statistics, *Cancer Facts & Figures 1995* (New York: The American Cancer Society, 1994); risk factors, *Harrison's Principles of Internal Medicine*, 12th ed., op. cit., p. 1621; survival rates, *Current Medical Diagnosis and Treatment 1993*, op. cit., p. 557; Boston Women's Collective, *The New Our Bodies, Ourselves* (New York: Simon & Schuster, 1992), p. 619; preventive removal of male breast, Health Gazette Medical News, *U.S. Pharmacist*, January 1994.

bruises: *The Merck Manual*, 16th ed., op. cit., p. 1207.

bulimia: Incidence statistics, *The Merck Manual*, 16th ed., op. cit., p. 2280; binge eating, calories consumed, Logue, *The Psychology of Eating and Drinking*, op. cit., p. 160; 1988 study, "Bulimia's binges linked to hormones," *Science News*, September 17, 1988.

bunions: Prevalence among girls, *Handbook of Pediatrics*, 16th ed., p. 812; definitions, treatment, Popovich, "Foot care products," *Handbook of Nonprescription Drugs*, 9th ed., op. cit., p. 996.

calcium: Absorption and bone growth, National Research Council, *Recommended Dietary Allowances*, 10th ed., op. cit., pp. 174–81 passim.

calories: National Research Council, *Recommended Dietary Allowances*, 10th ed., op. cit., pp. 24–31 passim.

cancer: Lifetime risk, American Cancer Society, *Cancer Facts & Figures, 1995*.

canker sores: *Current Medical Diagnosis and Treatment 1993*, op. cit., p. 170.

carpal tunnel syndrome: Female predominance, *Mayo Clinic Health Letter*, April 1990; *The Merck Manual*, 16th ed., op. cit., p. 1519.

cataract: Gender relationship, *The Merck Manual of Geriatrics*, William B. Abrams and Robert Berkow, eds. (Rahway, NJ: Merck, Sharp & Dohme Research Laboratories, 1990), p. 1126.

chocolate: Stimulants, Charles Zapsalis and R. Anderle Beck, *Food Chemistry and Nutritional Biochemistry* (New York: John Wiley & Sons, 1985), pp. 1042–46; fat, *Recommended Dietary Allowances*, op. cit., pp. 44–45; food preferences, Suzanne Hamlin, "It's hard to ignore cravings: Researchers can't resist," *New York Times*, February 22, 1995; fn., Carol Ann Rinzler, *The Signet Book of Chocolate* (New York: New American Library, 1977), pp. 7–8.

cholesterol: Men vs. women, "Effect of gender, age and lipid status on low density lipoprotein subfraction distribution," *Arteriosclerosis*, September–October 1987; cholesterol and penile arteries, interview, Arthur Burnett, January 1994.

chronic obstructive pulmonary disease: American Lung Association, *Lung Disease Data 1993*.

cirrhosis of the liver: Statistics, *Harrison's Principles of Internal Medicine*, 12th ed., op. cit., p. 1341; male/female enzyme production, "Study tells why alcohol is greater risk to women," *New York Times*, January 11, 1990, op. cit., and Mario Frezza et al., "High blood alcohol levels in women," *The New England Journal of Medicine*, January 11, 1988.

cleft palate: 1/100 births, multifactorial influences, *Columbia University College of Physicians and Surgeons Complete Home Medical Guide*, op. cit., p. 732.

cold, tolerance for: Muscle vs. fat, Beller, *Fat and Thin*, op. cit., p. 91; iron stores, *Medical World News*, June 13, 1988; Raynaud's, "Cold triggers Raynaud's phenomenon," University of Wisconsin–Madison press release, November 1988, and *Science News*, November 29, 1986; Dianne Ackermann, *The Natural History of the Senses* (N.Y.: Random House, 1993), p. 91.

color blindness: Statistics, Pinckney and Pinckney, *The Patient's Guide to Medical Tests*, op. cit., p. 62; genetics, *Current Medical Diagnosis and Treatment 1993*, op. cit., p. 1275.

conception and birth rates, male versus female: Conception rates, Smith, *The Body*, op. cit., p. 172; population statistics, male vs. female, Natalie Angier, "In sperm, men have prenatal advantage," *New York Times*, October 30, 1990; acid vaginal environment, *The New Our Bodies, Ourselves*, op. cit., p. 391.

corpus callosum: Larger isthmus, MRI imaging, stroke, "Subtle but intriguing differences found in the brain anatomy of men and women," *New York Times*, April 11, 1989; isthmus 23 percent larger, dyslexia, "Gray matters," *Newsweek*, March 27, 1995; Simon LeVay, *The Sexual Brain*, op. cit., pp. 99–100.

death, ten leading causes: *Harrison's Principles of Internal Medicine*, 12th ed., op. cit., p. 16.

death, time of: David P. Phillips et al., "The birthday: Lifeline or deadline?" *Psychosomatic Medicine*, 54:532–42, 1992.

depression: Statistics, male vs. female, *The Merck Manual*, 16th ed., op. cit., p. 1514–15; Robert M. Sapolsky, *Why Zebras Don't Get Ulcers* (New York: W. H. Freeman, 1994), pp. 215–17; PET scan, "Gray matters," *Newsweek*, March 27, 1995.

diabetes: *Columbia University College of Physicians and Surgeons Complete Home Medical Guide*, op. cit., pp. 516–17.

direction, finding: "Boys and girls are different: Men, women and the sex differences," John Stossel, *ABC News Special*, August 31, 1995; LeVay, *The Sexual Brain*, op. cit., pp. 99–100.

diverticulosis: *The Merck Manual*, 16th ed., op. cit., p. 555.

doctors, attitudes (male versus female): Edith Gross, "Gender differences in physicians' stress," *Journal of the American Medical Women's Association*, July–August 1992; Debra Roter et al., "Sex differences in patients' and physicians' communication during primary care medical visits," *Medical Care* v. 29, no. 11, pp. 1083–1093; Minnesota study, Nicole Lurie et al., "Preventive care for women, Does the sex of the physician matter," *The New England Journal of Medicine*, August 12, 1993.

doctors, ratio of male versus female: Percent of women doctors, Sam Roberts, "Women's work: What's new, what isn't," *New York Times*, April 27,

1995; number of female gynecologists, *New Woman*, April 1995; college freshman, *New York Times Magazine*, September 10, 1995.

Down's syndrome: Laurence E. Karp, "Older fathers and genetic mutations," op. cit.

DuPuytren's contracture: Description, *The Merck Manual*, 16th ed., op. cit., p. 1369; DuPuytren biography, *Stedman's Medical Dictionary*, 26th ed., op. cit., p. 527; male prevalence, *The Mayo Clinic Health Letter*, February 1990.

dyslexia: Intelligence, boys vs. girls, *The Merck Manual*, 16th ed., op. cit., p. 2106; *Science News*, October 22, 1994; corpus callosum, connections between hemispheres, "Gray matters," *Newsweek*, March 27, 1995; Simon LeVay, *The Sexual Brain*, op. cit., pp. 99–100.

ears   Smith, *The Body*, op. cit., p. 249.

eating disorders: *The Merck Manual*, 16th ed., op. cit., pp. 2279–80; boys similar to girls, Hilde Bruch, *Eating Disorders* (New York: Basic Books, 1973); p. 285; athletes, Harrison's Principles of Internal Medicine, 12th ed., op. cit., p. 418.

emotion: "Man's world, woman's world? Brain studies point to differences," *New York Times*, February 28, 1995.

exercise: Heart Association statistics, male vs. female, American Heart Association, *Heart and Stroke Facts, 1994 supplement* (Dallas: American Heart Association, 1994); NCHS statistics, "Prevention and treatment of osteoporosis in women," *U.S. Pharmacist*, supplement, September 1994; CDC statistics, "Lack of exercise cited in U.S. women," *New York Times*, February 19, 1995; exercise, bone density, amenorrhea, *New York Times*, and *Columbia University College of Physicians and Surgeons Complete Home Medical Guide,* op. cit., p. 541, injuries, *The Merck Manual*, 16th ed., op. cit., p. 2556.

eyebrows and eyelashes: *Harrison's Principles of Internal Medicine*, 12th ed., op. cit., p. 302.

eyelids, swollen: *The Mayo Clinic Health Letter*, December 1985.

Fabry's disease: *The Merck Manual*, 16th ed., op. cit., p. 1050.

fat: Female fleshiness, calipers, Beller, *Fat and Thin*, op. cit., pp. 57–58; first few months of life, National Research Council, *Recommended Dietary Allowances*, 10th ed., op. cit., p. 30; puberty/adulthood, Logue, *The Psychology of Eating and Drinking*, op. cit., p. 165; old age, *The Merck Manual*, 16th ed., op. cit., p. 2546; age and body weight, R. Andres et al., "Impact of age on weight goals," *Annals of Internal Medicine*, December 6, 1985; Michigan study, *Moxie*, April 1990, and *Science News*, January 9, 1988; adult fat/muscle comparison, Smith, *The Body*, op. cit., p. 508.

feet: Infancy, childhood, middle age, *Handbook of Nonprescription Drugs*, 9th ed., op. cit., p. 964.

fertility: Implanting of fertilized egg, *The World Book Health & Medical Annual* (Chicago: World Book, 1995), p. 315.

fetus, sex of: Testosterone, weight gains, hypertension, blood flow, Naeye and Tafari, *Risk Factors in Pregnancy and Diseases of the Fetus and Newborn*, op. cit., p. 314, p. 321; Kennedy baby, American Lung Association, *Lung Disease Data 1993*; surfactant, *New York Times*, March of Dimes Supplement, April 9, 1995.

finger length: Skeletal differences, Pat Shipman, Alan Walker, David Bichell, *The Human Skeleton* (Cambridge, MA: Harvard University Press, 1985), pp. 270–77; finger bones, Smith, *The Body*, op. cit., p. 504.

fingerprints: Smith, *The Body*, op. cit., p. 404.

food cravings: Male/female differences, Hamlin, "It's hard to ignore cravings: Researchers can't resist," *New York Times*, op. cit., February 22, 1995; pica, infant preferences, Logue, *The Psychology of Eating and Drinking*, op. cit., p. 84, p. 89.

fragile X syndrome: Characteristics, 1/2,000, *Current Medical Diagnosis and Treatment 1993*, op. cit., p. 1279; autism, *Harrison's Principles of Internal Medicine*, 12th ed., pp. 2057–58; *New York Times*, March of Dimes Supplement, April 9, 1995.

gallbladder disease: "Gallstones," *Clinical symposia*, CIBA-GEIGY, vol. 40, no. 2, 1988; statistics, "Gallstone Disease Fact Sheet," Lobsenz-Stevens, May 16, 1988, "Digestive disease national coalition urges early detection of gallstones," Digestive Disease National Coalition press release (n.d.), *U.S. Pharmacist*, supplement, op. cit., September 1994; fn., composition of bile, *Harrison's Principles of Internal Medicine*, 12th ed., op. cit., p. 1358.

germ cells: Fetal estrogen production, Harrison's Principles of Internal Medicine, 12th ed., op. cit., p. 1776; Laurence E. Karp, "Older fathers and genetic mutations," op. cit.; J. M. Friedman, "Genetic Diseases in the offspring of older fathers," op. cit.; production of sperm and egg, George Noland, *General Biology*, 11th ed. (St. Louis: C. V. Mosby, 1983), pp. 78–85 passim.

gout: *The Merck Manual*, 16th ed., op. cit., pp. 1346–47; 1/9, *Current Medical Diagnosis and Treatment 1993*, op. cit., p. 642; Hippocrates quote, *Arthritis Today*, January–February 1987.

Graves' disease: 7:1, *Harrison's Principles of Internal Medicine*, 12th ed., op. cit., p. 1703; 8:1, *Current Medical Diagnosis and Treatment 1993*, op. cit., p. 866.

growth: Age, height, weight, Merenstein et al., *Handbook of Pediatrics*, 16th ed., op. cit., p. 373; speed of growth, *The Merck Manual*, 16th ed., op. cit., p. 2273.

hair: Gain/loss in old age, Kligman et al., "Aging of Human Skin," *Handbook of the Biology of Aging*, 2nd ed., op. cit., p. 828; hairiest parts, receptors, Ackermann, *The Natural History of the Senses*, op. cit., p. 68; and Smith, *The Body*, op. cit., pp. 398–99.

hair, graying: "Biology: Rate of graying of human hair," *Nature*, August 21, 1965; inherited graying, not a health problem, Kligman et al., "Aging of Human Skin," *Handbook of the Biology of Aging*, 2nd ed., op. cit., p. 828.

hands, cold: Muscle vs. fat, energy production, National Research Council, *Recommended Dietary Allowances*, 10th ed., op. cit., pp. 25 ff.; Beller, *Fat and Thin*, op. cit., p. 91.

handwriting: "Q&A," *New York Times*, July 10, 1990.

Hansen's disease: *Harrison's Principles of Internal Medicine*, 12th ed., op. cit., pp. 645–646.

Hashimoto's disease: *The Merck Manual*, 16th ed., op. cit., p. 1083.

hay fever: *Percutaneous immediate hypersensitivity to eight allergens,* National Center for Health Statistics, series 11, n. 235, July 1986.

headache: Statistics, *U.S. Pharmacist,* January 1991; 15 percent, sinus headache, eyestrain, W. Kent Van Tyle, "Internal analgesic products," *Handbook of Nonprescription Drugs,* 9th ed., op. cit., pp. 58–59; cluster headaches, *The Merck Manual,* 16th ed., op. cit., p. 1423.

hearing: Interview with Robert Henkin.

hearing loss: *The Merck Manual,* 16th ed., op. cit., p. 2340.

heartbeat: Childhood heartbeat, Smith, *The Body,* op. cit., p. 285; normal adult pulse rate, *The Guinness Book of Records 1994,* op. cit., p. 180; blood quantities, *Man's Body,* op. cit., B13–15.

heart bypass surgery: *The Merck Manual of Geriatrics* (Rahway, NJ: Merck, Sharpe & Dohme Research Laboratories, 1990), p. 417.

heart disease: Death rates and definitions, American Heart Association, *Heart and Stroke Facts, 1994 supplement;* estrogen and male blood clots, Thomas J. Moore, *Heart Failure* (New York: Random House, 1989), p. 52; St. Luke's testosterone study, *Arteriosclerosis and Thrombosis,* Journal of the American Medical Association, May 1994; Heartstyle, American Heart Association, Fall 1994.

heart transplants: American Heart Association, *Heart and Stroke Facts, 1994 supplement;* pacemaker, "Pulsepoints," *American Health,* April 1995.

height: Median heights, National Research Council, *Recommended Dietary Allowances,* 10th ed., op. cit., endpaper chart; tallest, shortest, *Guinness Book of Records,* op. cit., pp. 146–48, p. 150; Boston studies, interviews with Patricia Hebert and Palme; Turner and Noonan syndromes, more boys in therapy, *Current Medical Diagnosis and Treatment,* op. cit., p. 842.

hemophilia: Prevalence and genetics, *The Merck Manual,* 16th ed., op. cit., p. 1218.

hiccups: Description, more common among men, *The Merck Manual,* 16th ed., op. cit, p. 1426; process, Rose, *The Body in Time,* op. cit., pp. 38–40; long-lasting hiccups, *The Guinness Book of Records,* op. cit., p. 177.

high blood pressure (hypertension):   *Harrison's Principles of Internal Medicine*, 12th ed., op. cit., p. 1002; higher male mortality, Naeye and Tafari, *Risk Factors in Pregnancy and Diseases of the Fetus and Newborn*, op. cit., p. 322; mortality statistics, American Heart Association, *Heart and Stroke Facts, 1994 Supplement*.

hip: Shipman et al., *The Human Skeleton*, op. cit., pp. 274–75; *The Visual Dictionary of the Human Body*, op. cit., pp. 14–15; *Smith, The Body*, op. cit., p. 213; 33 percent of women, 17 percent of men, *U.S. Pharmacist*, supplement, op. cit.

hip dislocation: *The Merck Manual*, 16th ed., op. cit., p. 2073; Merenstein et al., *Handbook of Pediatrics*, 16th ed., op. cit., pp. 794–95.

HIV (human immunodeficiency virus) infections: Symptoms, 7 to 40 percent transmission to baby, *The New Our Bodies, Ourselves*, op. cit., p. 327, p. 332, p. 336; transmission of HIV virus, "AIDS is now the leading killer of Americans from 25 to 44," *New York Times*, January 31, 1995; AZT in pregnancy, *FDA Medical Bulletin*, Food and Drug Administration, February 1995.

Hodgkin's disease: Statistics, Merenstein et al., *Handbook of Pediatrics*, 16th ed., op. cit., p. 924, and *The Merck Manual*, 16th ed., op. cit., p. 1245; genetic possibilities, *Harrison's Principles of Internal Medicine*, 12th ed., op. cit., p. 1609.

homicide victims: Statistics, U.S. Centers for Disease Control, "Provisional numbers of deaths for the 10 leading causes of death by age, race and sex, United States, 1992," *Monthly Vital Statistics*, September 28, 1993.

homosexuals, number of males versus females: Up to 10 percent of men, *The Merck Manual*, 16th ed., op. cit., p. 1572; Simon LeVay, *The Sexual Brain*, op. cit., pp. 107–8; John Matthews, "A question of sexual orientation," *ASU Research*, Arizona State University, Fall/Winter 1994.

ichthyosis: *The Merck Manual*, 16th ed., op. cit., p. 2446; Merenstein et al., *Handbook of Pediatrics*, 16th ed., op. cit., p. 551.

immune system: Immune system cells, *Stedman's Medical Dictionary*, 26th ed., op. cit.; differences in male/female immune systems, *Science News*, January 23, 1980; Lahita, *Arthritis Today*, January–February 1987.

immune system deficiency disorders, inherited: *The Merck Manual*, 16th ed., op. cit., pp. 280–310 passim.

infertility: *U.S. Pharmacist*, September 1994; *Harrison's Principles of Internal Medicine*, 12th ed., op. cit., pp. 1770–1773.

insomnia: Women complain more frequently, Charles Morin, *Insomnia* (New York: Guilford Press, 1993), p. 8, and Wilse B Webb, *Sleep: The Gentle Tyrant* (Bolton, MA: Arker Publishing, 1992), p. 81; meta-analysis of 43 studies, L. C. Lack, S. J. Thorn, "Sleep disorders: Their prevalence and behavioral treatment," in *International Perspectives in Behavioral Medicine*, vol. II (Norwood, NJ: Ablex Publishing, 1988); sleep and mood swings, Susan Ince, "Pillow Talk," *Mirabella*, April 1995.

iron, dietary requirements: Body stores, National Research Council, *Recommended Dietary Allowances*, 10th ed., op. cit., pp. 193–94, p. 200; *The Merck Manual*, 16th ed., op. cit., p. 1145, and *Current Medical Diagnosis and Treatment 1993*, op. cit., p. 399.

iron deficiency anemia: National Research Council, *Recommended Dietary Allowances*, 10th ed., op. cit., p. 293; *The Merck Manual*, 16th ed., op. cit., pp. 1147–48; protective low female iron levels, "Excess iron linked to heart disease," *Science News*, September 19, 1992.

iron overload: *Harrison's Principles of Internal Medicine*, 12th ed., op. cit., p. 1826.

irritable bowel syndrome: *The Merck Manual*, 16th ed., op. cit., pp. 839–41.

jawbones: Shipman et al., *The Human Skeleton*, op. cit., pp. 273–74.

jaw pain: Female predominance, interview with Martin Schwartz National Center for Stuttering, New York University School of Medicine; miscellaneous causes, *The Merck Manual*, 16th ed., op. cit., p. 2407.

Kaposi's sarcoma: *The Merck Manual Of Geriatrics*, op. cit., p. 1034; *The Merck Manual*, 16th ed., op. cit., p. 2460.

kidney cancer: American Cancer Society, *Cancer Facts & Figures, 1995.*

kidney infection: Statistics, National Center for Health Statistics, *Vital Statistics of the United States, 1991*, op. cit.

kidney stones: *Harrison's Principles of Internal Medicine*, 12th ed., op. cit., p. 1204.

language and speech: Definitions, *Harrison's Principles of Internal Medicine*, 12th ed., op. cit., p. 203; hemisphere size, corpus callosum, "Subtle but intriguing differences found in the brain anatomy of men and women," *New York Times*, April 11, 1989.

left-handedness: 95 percent, *Harrison's Principles of Internal Medicine*, 12th ed., op. cit., p. 203; early preference, *Columbia University College of Physicians and Surgeons Complete Home Medical Guide*, op. cit., p. 240; testosterone levels, C. M. McCormick, S. F. Witelson, E. Kingstone, "Left-handedness in homosexual men and women: Neuroendocrine implications," *Psychoneuroendocrinology*, 1990, and interaction between hemispheres, Simon LeVay, *The Sexual Brain*, op. cit., p. 119.

legs: Anatomy, Smith, *The Body*, op. cit., p. 504; Lewis, Joyner, records, *The Guinness Book of Records*, op. cit., p. 742.

leukemia: *Current Diagnosis and Treatment 1993*, op. cit., p. 428; CLL, *The Merck Manual*, 16th ed., op. cit., pp. 1241–42.

life expectancy: Men vs. women, older than 80, *The World Almanac and Book of Facts 1994*, op. cit., p. 958; U.S. life expectancy, Rose, *The Body in Time*, op. cit., p. 169; Japan, *The Guinness Book of Records, 1994*, op. cit., p. 458; Mlle. Calment, *The Guinness Book of Records*, op. cit., p. 159, and *Newsweek*, March 6, 1995.

lipoproteins: Age-related changes, *Harrison's Principles of Internal Medicine*, 12th ed., op. cit., p. 75; Judith R. Macnamara, et al., "Effect of gender, age and lipid status on low density lipoprotein subfraction distribution," *Arteriosclerosis*, September–October 1987; statistics, American Heart Association, *Heart and Stroke Facts, 1994 supplement*.

liver: Bilirubin, four-month life of blood cell, Pinckney and Pinckney, *The Patient's Guide to Medical Tests*, op. cit., p. 25; *Harrison's Principles of Internal Medicine*, 12th ed., op. cit., p. 1316, p. 1320.

liver cancer: American Cancer Society, *Cancer Facts and Figures 1995*.

lung cancer: Statistics, new cases, deaths, American Cancer Society, *Cancer Facts and Figures 1995*; increase in lung cancer rates, American Lung Association, *Lung Disease Data 1993*.

lungs: Premature boys, Naeye and Tafari, *Risk Factors in Pregnancy and Diseases of the Fetus and Newborn*, op. cit., p. 309; early infections, *The Merck Manual*, 16th ed., op. cit., p. 2025; lung function, disease data, American Lung Association, *Lung Disease Data 1993*; blood flow, conversion factors, liters to gallons (1.06), *Stedman's Medical Dictionary*, 26th ed., op. cit.

macular degeneration: More common in women, *Current Diagnosis and Treatment 1993*, op. cit., p. 138; no gender difference, *The Merck Manual*, 16th ed., op. cit., p. 2385.

magnesium: National Research Council, *Recommended Dietary Allowances*, 10th ed., op. cit., pp. 189–91; average consumption, *Good Sources of Nutrients* (Washington, D.C.: USDA, Human Nutrition Services, January 1990); CP babies, "Infant CP protection," *Science News*, February 25, 1995.

Marfan's syndrome: *The Merck Manual*, 16th ed., op. cit., pp. 2251–52; Laurence E. Karp "Older fathers and genetic mutations," op. cit.

marriage: San Francisco study, "New twist to marriage and mortality," *Science News*, October 27, 1990; "Marriage is a lifesaver for men after 45," *New York Times*, October 16, 1990; older women, *The Guinness Book of Records*, op. cit., p. 158.

mathematical skills: "Gray matters," *Newsweek*, March 27, 1995.

measles: *The Merck Manual*, 16th ed., op. cit., p. 2171.

Meniere's syndrome: *Columbia University College of Physicians and Surgeons Home Medical Guide*, op. cit., p. 717; *Current Medical Diagnosis and Treatment 1993*, op. cit., p. 158.

migraine: Statistics, *U.S. Pharmacist*, January 1991; birth control pills, *Current Medical Diagnosis and Treatment 1993*, p. 586, early adolescence, p. 729; menstrual cycle, *New Woman*, November 1994; cluster headaches, *The Merck Manual*, 16th ed., op. cit., p. 1423.

miscarriage: *Columbia University College of Physicians and Surgeons Complete Home Medical Guide*, op. cit., p. 201; *The Merck Manual*, 16th ed., op. cit., p. 1866.

motion sickness: Women, interview with Stephen Harner, M.D., consultant at the Mayo Clinic; *Mayo Clinic Health Letter*, April 1987; "Dizzyness and Motion Sickness," The American Academy of Otolaryngology–Head and Neck Surgery, February 1990.

multiple sclerosis: Interview, The National Multiple Sclerosis Society; The Merck Manual, 16th ed., op. cit., p. 1488.

muscle: Definitions, *The Visual Dictionary of the Human Body*, op. cit., p. 22; testosterone/muscle, *Columbia University College of Physicians and Surgeons Complete Home Medical Guide*, op. cit., p. 254.

muscular dystrophy: *The Merck Manual*, 16th ed., op. cit., p. 1526.

myasthenia gravis: Merenstein et al., *Handbook of Pediatrics*, 16th ed., op. cit., p. 852; age of onset, *The Merck Manual*, 16th ed., op. cit., p. 1524.

neck: Muscles, *The Visual Dictionary of the Human Body*, op. cit., p. 25; interview, Robert K. Watson, New Haven Sleep Disorders Center; Adam's apple, *Stedman's Medical Dictionary*, 26th ed. (Baltimore: Williams & Wilkins, 1995); growth rate, voice and penis, Smith, *The Body*, op. cit., p. 292.

nightmares: Incidence, Marrku Partinen, "Epidemiology of sleep disorders," *Principles and Practices of Sleep Medicine*, op. cit.; sleep patterns, Rose, *The Body In Time*, op. cit., p. 95; children, Merenstein et al., *The Handbook of Pediatrics*, 16th ed., op. cit., p. 844.

obesity: The Institute of Medicine, press release, February 19, 1995; Beller, *Fat and Thin*, op. cit., p. 59.

oral cancers: American Cancer Society, *Cancer Facts & Figures 1994*.

organ transplants: "Finding the gene for a female attack," *Science News*, August 26, 1995.

orgasm: Muscle reactions, *The Merck Manual*, 16th ed., op. cit. p. 1573; resolution, *Harrison's Principles of Internal Medicine,* 12th ed., op. cit., p. 296; simultaneous orgasm, Rose, *The Body in Time*, op. cit., p. 10.

osteoporosis: Types of bones, *The Merck Manual*, 16th ed., op. cit., p. 1357; statistics on posture, *U.S. Pharmacist* supplement, September 1994, op. cit.; rate of fractures, National Osteoporosis Foundation, *Osteoporosis Fact Sheet*, (n.d.).; studies, *Newsday* (New York), October 23, 1993.

pain: Different perceptions of pain, Smith, *The Body*, op. cit., pp. 158–59; endorphins in pregnancy, Ackermann, *The Natural History of the Senses*, op. cit., pp. 105–6; endorphins in placentae, *The New Our Bodies, Ourselves*, op. cit., p. 448; placebo effect, Van Tyle, "Internal analgesic products," *Handbook of Nonprescription Drugs*, op. cit., p. 58.

pancreatic cancer: Statistics, American Cancer Society, *Cancer Facts & Figures 1995, and Cancer Risk Report: Prevention and Control, 1994*; changes that lead to tumors in animals, University of Texas Southwestern Medical Center press release, August 25, 1993.

pelvis: Shipman et al., *The Human Skeleton*, op. cit., pp. 274–75.

perspiration: Hormones, George M. Briggs and Doris Howes Callaway, *Nutrition and Physical Fitness*, 11th ed. (New York: Holt, Rinehart and Winston, 1984), p. 113, p. 114; different sweat glands, function, Miller et al., "Personal care products," *Handbook of Nonprescription Drugs*, 9th ed., op. cit., p. 754; complex mixture, American Chemical Society, August 28, 1990, op. cit., interview with George Preti; interview with Dawn French, Proctor and Gamble.

physical strength: Smith, *The Body*, op. cit., p. 14.

pneumonia and influenza: *Harrison's Principles of Internal Medicine*, 12th ed., op. cit., p. 16.

population: 1900 U.S. population, Census figures, persons older than 80, *The World Almanac and Book of Facts 1994*, op. cit., p. 958; world figures, *The Guinness Book of Records*, op. cit., p. 454; 4 to 1, *Man's Body*, op. cit., p. A32; divorce risk, "Temptation may make heart rove, study finds," *The New York Times*, February 19, 1995.

porphyrias: *The Merck Manual*, 16th ed., op. cit., p. 1032.

pregnancy: Ectopic pregnancy, *The Merck Manual*, 16th ed., op. cit., p. 1768; abdominal pregnancy, *The New Our Bodies, Ourselves*, op. cit., p. 246; Teresi article, *New York Times Magazine*, November 27, 1994.

protein: National Research Council, *Recommended Dietary Allowances*, 10th ed., op. cit.

puberty: Signs of puberty, *The Merck Manual*, 16th ed., op. cit., p. 2274, p. 2275; girls reach puberty first, Catholic Church, Rose, *The Body In Time*, op. cit., p. 163, p. 164; voice cracking, Smith, *The Body*, op. cit., p. 292; age of menarche, precocious puberty, *Handbook of Pediatrics*, 16th ed., op. cit., p. 373, p. 865.

quinine: *The Physicians' Desk Reference*, 48th ed. (Montvale, NJ: Medical Economics, 1994), pp. 695, 1317, 1923, 2085, 2087, 2113.

Raynaud's disease: *Current Medical Diagnosis and Treatment 1993*, op. cit., pp. 383–84; *The Merck Manual*, 16th ed., op. cit., pp. 583–84; catecholamines, *Stedman's Medical Dictionary*, 26th ed; "Cold triggers Raynaud's phenomenon," University of Wisconsin–Madison press release, November 1988.

reading: Reading and brain use, "Man's world, woman's world? Brain studies point to differences," *New York Times*, February 28, 1995; "Gray matters," *Newsweek*, March 27, 1995.

red blood cells: *Current Medical Diagnosis and Treatment 1993*, op. cit., p. 400.

reproductive hazards: Female hazards, Carol Ann Rinzler, *The Safe Pregnancy Book* (New York: New American Library, 1984), pp. 115–31; "Study finds sperm counts are declining," *New York Times*, February 2, 1995; "Sperm changes linked to drinking water," *Science News*, February 26, 1994; "Court backs right of women to jobs with health risks," *New York Times*, March 21, 1991; "Equal rights, equal risks," *Newsweek*, April 1, 1991, "Dad's farming may hike baby's liver risk," *Science News*, July 6, 1991; Jane Brody, "Possible links are being explored between babies' health and fathers' habits and working conditions," *New York Times*, December 25, 1991; "The sins of the fathers," *Newsweek*, November 26, 1990.

reproductive organs: TDF, Wolffian/Müllerian glands, organ formation, *Harrison's Principles of Internal Medicine*, 12th ed., op. cit., pp. 1799–1800;

comparisons, *Columbia University College of Physicians and Surgeons Complete Home Medical Guide*, op. cit., p. 202; *Stedman's Medical Dictionary*, 26th ed., op. cit.

rheumatic heart disease: Statistics, American Heart Association, *Heart and Stroke Facts, 1994 supplement.*

scoliosis: *Handbook of Pediatrics*, 16th ed., op. cit., p. 800; definitions, *Stedman's Medical Dictionary*, 26th ed., op. cit.; juvenile scoliosis, *Columbia University College of Physicians and Surgeons Complete Home Medical Guide*, op. cit., p. 594.

sebaceous glands: Kligman et al., "Aging of Human Skin," *Handbook of the Biology of Aging*, 2nd ed., op. cit., pp. 827–28.

selenium: National Research Council, *Recommended Dietary Allowances*, op. cit., p. 218, p. 220.

sex chromosomes: TDF, *Harrison's Principles of Internal Medicine*, 12th ed., op. cit., p. 1799; testosterone effects, Simon LeVay, *The Sexual Brain* op. cit., p. 22; aneuploidy, *Current Medical Diagnosis and Treatment 1993*, op. cit., p. 1277.

sex hormones: Testosterone conversion, *Harrison's Principles of Internal Medicine*, 12th ed., op. cit., p. 75; progesterone, *Columbia University College of Physicians and Surgeons Complete Home Medical Guide*, op. cit., p. 201; cartilage/bone, *Visual Dictionary of the Human Body*, op. cit., p. 14.

sexual arousal: Physical events leading to arousal, sexual problems, *The Merck Manual*, 16th ed., op. cit., p. 1573, pp. 1575–1581; breast-feeding, additional female orgasms, *The New Our Bodies, Ourselves*, op. cit., p. 400, p. 169.

shoulders: Bones and muscles, *Harrison's Principles of Internal Medicine*, 12th ed., op. cit., p. 1769–1770; throwing, Smith, *The Body*, op. cit., p. 504.

skeleton: Estrogen, testosterone, definitions, number of bones, Smith, *The Body*, op. cit., p. 504, p. 505; indicators, Shipman et al., *The Human Skeleton*, op. cit., p. 273.

skin: Weight, *Columbia University College of Physicians and Surgeons Complete Home Medical Guide*, op. cit., p. 658; skin thickness, Kligman et al., "Aging of human skin," *Handbook of the Biology of Aging*, 2nd ed., op. cit., p. 822; skin size, *Man's Body*, op. cit., p. D02.

skin tags: Kligman et al. "Aging of human skin," *Handbook of the Biology of Aging*, 2nd ed., op. cit., p. 822.

skull: Shipman et al., *The Human Skeleton*, op. cit., pp. 273–74.

sleep: Sleep time, Marrku Partinen, "Epidemiology of sleep disorders," *Principles and Practices of Sleep Medicine*, op. cit., passim; Bureau of Economic Research data, "Sleep? Why? There's no money in it," *New York Times*, August 2, 1989; sleep patterns and movement, Charles Moran, *Insomnia* (New York: Guilford Press, 1993), pp. 8–9; characteristics of female sleep, Susan Ince, "Pillow Talk," *Mirabella*, April 1995; REM sleep, Charles Reynolds, "Sleep of healthy seniors: A revisit," *Sleep*, vol. 8, no. 1, 1985; couples' sleep behavior, Association of Professional Sleep Societies press release, July 29, 1994.

sleep apnea: "Sleep disorder harms concentration, memory," Association of Professional Sleep Societies, press release, July 8, 1987; male predominance, *Mayo Clinic Health Letter*, February 1990; hormones, American Lung Association, *Lung Disease Data, 1993*; American Heart Association press release, 1990.

sleepwalking: 15 percent, *The Merck Manual*, 16th ed., op. cit., p. 2096; Marrku Partinen, "The epidemiology of sleep disorders," *Principles and Practices of Sleep Medicine*, op. cit.; interviews with Mittler, Ferber.

smell, sense of: Hormone production, male/female acuity, interview, Robert Henkin, and Ackermann, *The Natural History of the Senses*, op. cit., p. 44; anosmia, Kallmann's syndrome, *The Merck Manual*, 16th ed., op. cit., p. 1057, p. 2347, *Stedman's Medical Dictionary*, 26th ed., op. cit., and Simon LeVay, *The Sexual Brain*, op. cit., p. 94.

smokers: Trends, 44 million, American Cancer Society, *Cancer Facts & Figures 1995*; % of male and female smokers, American Heart Association, *Heart and Stroke Facts, 1994 supplement*; fewer female smokers, "Study shows drop in number of female smokers," *New York Times*, December 23, 1994; increase in young smokers, "White women show rise in smoking among young," *New York Times*, November 6, 1994.

smoking, effects of: Death rates for smokers, American Cancer Society, *Cancer Facts & Figures 1995*; pain reduction, "Cigarette smoking decreases ability to perceive pain," American Heart Association news release, November 14, 1990; menstrual discomfort, "Smoking worsens menstrual pain," *Science News*, July 23, 1994; "Mom's smoking linked to hearing defect," *Science News*, July 10, 1993; reduced estrogen production, *Mayo Clinic Health Letter*, April 1987; narrowed fetal airways, American Lung Association, *Lung Disease Data 1993*; penile arteries, "Study links smoking to impotence cases," *New York Times*, May 21, 1991.

snoring: Marrku Partinen, "The epidemiology of sleep disorders," *Principles and Practices of Sleep Medicine*, op. cit.

spatial reasoning: Different test performances, Simon LeVay, *The Sexual Brain*, op. cit., pp. 99–100, 117–18; hemisphere size, "Subtle but intriguing differences found in the brain anatomy of men and women," *New York Times*, April 11, 1989.

stillbirths: Blood flow to placenta, birth order, Naeye and Tafari, *Risk Factors in Pregnancy and Diseases of the Fetus and Newborn*, op. cit., p. 317; race, blood group, radiated, very old, Smith, *The Body*, p. 172, p. 173.

stomach cancer: American Cancer Society, *Cancer Facts & Figures 1995*.

stroke: American Heart Association, *Heart and Stroke Facts, 1994 supplement*; female advantage, "Men and women use brain differently, study discovers," *New York Times*, February 16, 1995; "Subtle but intriguing differences found in the brain anatomy of men and women," *New York Times*, April 11, 1989.

stuttering: Interview with Martin Schwartz, National Center for Stuttering.

suicide: Statistics, U.S. Centers for Disease Control, "Provisional numbers of deaths for the 10 leading causes of death by age, race and sex, United States, 1992," *Monthly Vital Statistics*, September 28, 1993, and National Center for Health Statistics, *Vital Statistics of the United States, 1991* (Washington, D.C.: Public Health Service, 1994); San Diego study, University of California–San Diego press release, September 12, 1992; adolescent suicides, *Handbook of Pediatrics*, 16th ed., op. cit., p. 376; success rate, *Man's Body*, op. cit., pp. B60–62; guns vs. poison, males vs. females, *The Merck Manual*, 16th ed., op. cit., p. 2272.

swimming: Fat vs. muscle, National Research Council, *Recommended Dietary Allowances*, 10th ed., op. cit., p. 30; male vs. female, "Females are better swimmers," *Science News*, December 14, 1974.

systemic lupus erythematosis: *The Merck Manual*, 16th ed., op. cit., pp. 1317–18.

target areas: Interview with Martin Schwartz; see individual entries for target areas.

teeth: Well-known people born with teeth, Smith, *The Body*, op. cit., p. 410, and *The Guinness Book of Records*, op. cit., p. 165; when teeth erupt, Rose, *The Body in Time*, op. cit., p. 157; interview with Michael Robert.

temperature: Fahrenheit, H. Arthur Klein, *The World of Measurements* (New York: Simon & Schuster, 1974), pp. 298–303; *The Merck Manual*, 16th ed., op. cit., p. 2490; 98.4 vs. 98.1, "What's normal? Would you believe 98.2?" *New York Times*, September 24, 1992.

thumb pain: *Mayo Clinic Health Letter*; Arthur Freese, "The arthritis gender gap," *Arthritis Today*, January–February 1987.

twins: Naeye, op. cit., p. 263; 1/80 births, *Columbia University College of Physicians and Surgeons Complete Home Medical Guide*, op. cit., p. 212; Siamese twins, Smith, *The Body*, op. cit., p. 203; Chang and Eng, *The Guinness Book of Records*, op. cit., pp. 155–56; death of, Frederick Drimmer, *Very Special People* (New York: Bantam Books, 1976), p. 26.

type A behavior: *Columbia University College of Physicians and Surgeons Complete Home Medical Guide*, op. cit., p. 346.

ulcers: "Duodenal ulcers," *Mayo Clinic Health Letter*, September 1989; *Harrison's Principles of Internal Medicine*, 12th ed., op. cit., pp. 1232–33; "Bacterium that causes ulcers discovered in drinking water," *New York Times*, May 24, 1995.

urinary tract infections: *The Merck Manual*, 16th ed., op. cit., p. 2154.

urine: Composition, volume, *The Merck Manual*, 16th ed., op. cit., p. 1647, p. 1652, p. 1952; *Diagnostic Tests Handbook*, op. cit., p. 238, p. 240, p. 273;

Pinckney and Pinckney, *The Patient's Guide To Medical Tests*, op. cit., p. 277–8; conversion, 17-0HCS, *Stedman's Medical Dictionary*, 26th ed., op. cit.

urine, flow rate: *Diagnostic Tests Handbook*, ed. Regina Daley Ford (Springhouse, PA: Springhouse Corporation, 1988), p. 660.

varicose veins: Landau, "Varicose veins," *U.S. Pharmacist*, July 1989; hormonal changes in pregnancy, *The Merck Manual*, 16th ed., op. cit., p. 590, and interview, Ronald Dee, Albert Einstein College of Medicine, New York.

vitamin A: National Research Council, *Recommended Dietary Allowances*, 10th ed., op. cit., pp. 84–85.

vitamin B complex: National Research Council, *Recommended Dietary Allowances*, op. cit., pp. 132–65 passim; folic acid, "Study finds vitamin reduces birth defects," *New York Times*, July 19, 1991; "Advice unheeded on averting birth defect," *New York Times*, March 4, 1995.

vitamin C: National Research Council, *Recommended Dietary Allowances*, op. cit., p. 118–19; smoking and vitamin C, "Smoking depletes vitamin C from mom, fetus," *Science News*, May 20, 1995.

vitamin D: National Research Council, *Recommended Dietary Allowances*, op. cit., p. 96.

vitamin E: National Research Council, *Recommended Dietary Allowances*, op. cit., pp. 99–105.

voice: Human voices, Ackermann, *The Natural History of the Senses*, op. cit., pp. 188–89; 125 cycles per second, Smith, *The Body*, op. cit., p. 360; loudness records, *The Guinness Book of Records*, op. cit., p. 170, p. 172; whisper and conversational tones, H. Arthur Klein, *The World of Measurements* (New York: Simon & Schuster, 1979), pp. 586–87, p. 604.

vocal cords: Growth of vocal cords, Smith, *The Body*, op. cit., p. 363; church choirs, Rose, *The Body in Time*, op. cit., p. 163.

walking: Skeletal structure, Shipman et al., *The Human Skeleton*, op. cit., pp. 274–75; *The Visual Dictionary of the Human Body*, op. cit., pp. 14–15; *The Body*, op. cit., p. 213; walking records, *The Guinness Book of Records*, op. cit., p. 765.

water: Muscle/fat, *U.S. Pharmacist*, March 1985; eight glasses of water, Carol Ann Rinzler, *Feed a Cold, Starve a Fever* (New York: Facts on File, 1991), p. 205; 30 minutes to an hour, Rose, *The Body in Time*, op. cit., p. 148; cell fluid, pregnancy, energy requirements, National Research Council, *Recommended Dietary Allowances*, op. cit., p. 20.

weight: Male/female weight difference, Smith, *The Body*, p. 295; median weights, National Research Council, *Recommended Dietary Allowances*, op. cit.; records, *The Guinness Book of Records*, op. cit., p. 151.

white blood cells: *Current Medical Diagnosis and Treatment 1993*, op. cit., p. 400.

wrinkles: Kligman et al., "Aging of Human Skin," *Handbook of the Biology of Aging*, 2nd ed. op. cit., pp. 828–29.

X-linked traits: *The World Book Health and Medical Annual 1995*, op. cit., pp. 223–24; general characteristics of an X-linked trait, *Current Medical Diagnosis and Treatment 1993*, op. cit., pp. 1275–76; Fabry's disease, *The Merck Manual*, 16th ed., op. cit., p. 1050.

yeast infections: *Current Medical Diagnosis and Treatment 1993*, op. cit., pp. 1169–70; *The Merck Manual*, 16th ed., op. cit., pp. 2422–23.

zinc: National Research Council, *Recommended Dietary Allowances*, op. cit., p. 209; zinc and male fitness, *Men's Fitness*, May 1994; largest store in testes, Pinckney and Pinckney, *The Patient's Guide to Medical Tests*, op. cit., p. 292.

INDEX

This index is designed to be used as a guide to the dictionary topics. The A-to-Z entries are indicated by **boldface** page references. The general subjects are subdivided by the A-to-Z entries. Page references followed by 't' indicate tables.